Onwards

Onwards

PUSHING 60

There are 100 numbered copies,
signed by the author.

———

For Hedwig and Chris
with appreciation
and love
Marcia xx

November 2021

MARCIA FARQUHAR

PUSHING 60

BOOKARTBOOKSHOP

Published by Bookartbookshop, 17 Pitfield st., London N1 6HB
©2021 Marcia Farquhar

Printed and bound by CPI, Chippenham.

Photo credits: Peggy Atherton 58 (2020); Coco (Visionary Underground) 50 (2006); Hydar Dewachi 46 (2013); E.J. Farquhar 16 (1973); John Farquhar 31 (1966), 42 (1957); Marcia Farquhar 1 (2014), 4 (2014), 10 (2014), 11 (2018), 13 (2019); Ella Finer 22 (2020); Jem Finer 3 (2020), 5 (2020), 6 (2020), 9 (2017), 12 (2016), 15 (2003), 17 (2020), 19 (2015), 20 (2020), 21 (2018), 21 (2021), 25 (2020), 27 (2020), 34 (2020), 35 (2020), 39 (1999), 40 (2020), 41 (2020), 43 (2020), 44 (2015), 48 (2020), 53 (2015), 54 (2021), 55 (2018), 57 (2020), 59 (2020), 60 (2018); Kitty Finer 23 (2021); Juan Guzmán 2, we were unable to trace the owners of the reproduction rights for this photograph, nor for Rafael Jáuregui 1; Jazz Mellor 47 (2021); Andrew Ranken 49; photographer unknown: 7, 8, 18, 26, 28, 33, 36, 45 (2013).

Many thanks to Lucio A. C. Shala, the first Arthole Artist's Award patron. The Arthole Award was conceived for LADA by the artist Joshua Sofaer in collaboration with Gary Carter, and enabled 2016's *Audio Arthole*, a year long weekly act of spontaneous speech, and 2017's *Pushing 60*, a sixty-day series of readings.

In a work of so called non-fiction there is no prolepsis, no flash forward; the future is an unknown and the past is a fiction, however much it gets called real.

I look back and I can see the future.

This piece of writing that has become *Pushing 60* began in 2014, as a response to an invitation to write 60 chapters about 'anything'.

As I didn't have a special subject, I thought of the number 60, and coming up to the age of sixty. I proposed a looking forwards and backwards.

I started in earnest and lasted for 10 chapters, then the commitment vanished. I don't even remember why I stopped.

I do not wish to overwhelm what follows with explanations, but I do want to identify the two different time zones of the following 60 chapters. The first ten were written to be read in print in 2014. The subsequent 50 were written daily between 8 November 2017 and 6 January 2018, the eve of my 60th birthday.

They were only ever written to be heard. I was addressing listeners.

When Tanya Peixoto invited me to be published by bookartbookshop she offered me the editorial skills of Alastair Brotchie of Atlas Press. He appears unnamed in *Pushing 60*, as someone who answers my rhetorical question as to whether mentioning meeting a superstar in a dream counts as name-dropping. He shouted out the answer: that it most certainly did. This decisive tendency has always impressed me.

Curiously the dream encounter came true very shortly after I had turned 60, at the birthday of an old friend.

When I did meet the legend, he offered me his seat and smiled as I brushed ash off our dear friend. He altered the angle of a mirror as I found my reflection distracting and kindly gave me a roll-up. It was my last cigarette. The liquorice paper was too sweet for me. I gave up that night. A dream come true.

I noticed the same black cigarette in a photo of Johnny Depp outside the courts last summer.

I feel fortunate that my own flailing and failing has not been the stuff of tabloids and rags.

I consider privacy and its pleasures, ageing and even writing, anonymously, and I know there is much to cherish. I have long hidden behind lost scripts. But the alarming honour of being offered such a fine writer to edit me is an offer I cannot refuse. I accept, but I think of Miss Scrivener, my English teacher, writing across my essays, 'I cannot bear to go on,' and giving me terrible marks because of my punctuation.

I met Miss Scrivener again in the early eighties. I'd just had my first child. She seemed a bit disappointed, and said she had expected to have heard of me being published 'by now'.

'What?' I said in real surprise, 'You of all people, who never finished my essays.'

'I always did,' she said, 'but there was something so unbearable about your punctuation.'

Here in Spain again, listening to the sea in the dark, I remember Miss Scrivener and Mrs Lazarus. Not just wonderful names but also…

Prudence Scrivener is dead. I wanted to visit her a few years ago. I met one of her friends, in publishing as it happens, at a church hall meeting for the elderly of the parish. 'She won't know you,' said the friend, 'Her mind has gone.' 'I don't need to be known,' I said, 'I know her and can tell her stories. She liked my stories as long as she didn't have to read them. She couldn't bear my punctuation.' The friend has gone now too.

My mother lives on, at least I think she does. I try not to wait for the call to say she has gone. She does not know who I am, and when she sees me on a screen I am her dead sister Marcia. 'She has had a tragic life but looks well for a woman of over 100,' she tells the kind young man who has given us this weekly opportunity to be remote together via Zoom.

'Her first husband was decapitated in Burma,' she says matter of factly, 'but then she married Jeremy Finer who is a well-respected physiotherapist.'

On the subject of names, I am not consistent in *Pushing 60*. Some, like Jem Finer, who is my husband but not a physiotherapist, are named, as is my friend Katy who I have known since I was five. But others are given initials and I can't quite fathom my motives now. I think Sophie is SR, as I'm not sure she will want me to tell unknown others what she has said. MH is given initials because of my mother's affection for him. Why am I so coy? I do not know why Debsey is DW and I can't think on reading it over in the last week how so many people who mean so much in my life simply do not appear.

I take out some stories about Jem's father that I think are Jem's stories more than mine. He appreciates this, and I wonder with some concern whether I am doing what I complain about others doing to me, nicking lines, story lines. I am not just taking lines but whole stories. Whole stories is an exaggeration, I remember only fragments.

The act of remembering takes place in time and space, and I muse on how the times and spaces impact on memories. All very obvious stuff but I am trying to remember again, now in Spain, where this whole thing started. What I once called 'the chronicles'.

My mother happy, looking out to sea in 2014. I read over the early pages, back to her wilfully gentle state and remember that I gave her a book on Pompeii. What a strange subject to inflict on an old person who only wanted to look out to sea and think happy thoughts. 'Here, mother, read about a terrifying event, a horror story that ends in total devastation.' Why would I give her such a book to read?

I am sorry for so many things that are too late. Among ghosts.

Long ago in 1999 I made a performance using a rack of clothes and the memories they evoked, and when asked if I would do it again, replied that I would do it every seven years for the rest of my life. I anticipated it coming of age on 1 November 2020 and how I would be over sixty. I imagined this date back then and wondered where I would be performing. I always thought that I would mark the occasion.

I was invited to revive this piece of work in November 2018, so at least I have been a 60-year-old up on the catwalk. The absence of a 21st birthday performance is easier to bear thanks to Judith Carlton's invitation to perform *Acts of Clothing* on its 19th anniversary at Dilston Grove. It was first performed at the South London Gallery, and the young man who helped put up my catwalk in 1999 is now the head of the Slade.

On the night of the 2018 performance of *Acts of Clothing* a show was opening at the South London Gallery on humour. I was surrounded by an audience of such legendary wits that I laughed at the thought of a show on humour opening without them.

The word '*duende*' of which I write in *Pushing 60* is not going to get a note. It is untranslatable but I compare it to 'spirit'. I think I make it mean what I want it to mean, not unlike Lewis Carroll's imperious egg Humpty Dumpty. The ghosts of Dilston Grove are bringing pleasure to my sleepless night. To name many of them would definitely be name-dropping.

There are many asides to this problem in *Pushing 60*.

Naming names. AB suggested a cast list might make the work more accessible. Instead we agreed on endnotes. AB doesn't know if 'PG' might need explanation, or 'geyser' even. The archaic terms of a boarding house can be left we decided, as they would be in a performance, unless someone shouted out 'What's a PG?' and then I'd tell them.

A PG is, or was, a paying guest. My brother and I sneered at the initials with disdain. We grand fictional youth looked down on such boarding-house terms. A geyser is a type of gas water heater with flames. I was embarrassed by the geyser. None of my friends would have known what a geyser was even if one had blown off the wall and hit them in the face.

AB notes that I get the dates of the Beckett plays at the Royal Court wrong and says Jean Genet was sadly not a Satrap in the Collège de 'Pataphysique. And on it goes. AB is so knowledgeable as to give me pages of suggestions, and to be fine when I leave odd usage in place. For example, I use 'romance' as a verb. I get it from my mother. I don't look it up and decide not to use his editorial suggestion of the more familiar verb, to 'romanticise'.

We agree if I go back and correct too much then it will no longer be a daily piece of writing in my voice. In one chapter I berate myself for having used the word 'loyalty' so thoughtlessly in the previous one. This only makes sense if you know that the chapters were written to be read aloud daily in one go on live radio. 'I am so sorry,' I say, 'for having been so self-aggrandising yesterday in the way I referred to my brother's schizophrenia.'

I had mentioned that when, in the early seventies, people visited my brother in Banstead, a Victorian asylum, he told visitors he was afraid that I was being reared to be the bride of Prince Charles.

Since writing *Pushing 60* I went to a school reunion. When I recalled my brother's fear, Hermione 'Minnie' Kenyon, as pretty as ever, shot back, 'Well he dodged a bullet.'

I laughed a schoolgirl-laugh at the thought of myself as the bullet Prince Charles dodged.

To Jean

PUSHING 60

Endnotes are marked with an asterisk and can be found on pp.202-216.
Captions to pictures are ordered clockwise from top left,
the numbers refer to chapter numbers.
Use the QR code to hear Marcia Farquhar reading this version of *Pushing 60*.

1

I lost the first chapter. It probably wasn't as good as I imagine. Now it has vanished it can be romanced. But it was a start. My sideways thumb is numb, but I'll start again as my aim is to carry on…

Happy Sisyphus.

I can't stop now. I have accepted the challenge to write 60 chapters on whatever, for whoever. I was invited by Sandra Bartoli★, whose essays on the Tiergarten were so riveting that I read them in one sitting.

A hard act to follow.

It's my birthday and I'm approaching 60. It's a starry dark hour before dawn; the light on my phone is as bright as neon. I consider the meaning of 60 and realise it's already on my mind. Today I will be 56 and so nearer to 60 than 50. The theme has come. I will write about ageing and change, and any old thing.

Looking forwards and backwards like Janus, I can hear the sea. It's gentle this early morning and I can hear the breathing beside me. The breathing is also gentle. I have known the breather beside me for well over 30 years. I think of Winnie in *Happy Days*, keeping going while her silent husband lies behind the rock. I think of being beached and *for how much longer*…

My last breath is conscious. I think about the last breath – never knowingly taken – as I pull air in to my lungs and consider giving up smoking.

'They gave me up,' my mother says cheerfully. She is with us on this birthday trip. I was nearly given away. But I was kept. My sister says it was because I was a suck-up. What an idiot baby.

'I got my family for free!' I would joke with the German analyst when I complained about the agony of paying so much money. That was a poor joke, and neither of us laughed. 'But you weren't given away,' she would remind me.

I am in Spain where I first came as a girl in '77, inspired by Lorca and revolutionary Spaniards in punk time London. I wanted to be the girl on the roof of the Colón in Barcelona but I was just a 'little bourgeois' so my Spanish *novio*,★ told me, until I cried, which made him laugh.

He is now a teacher in a nearby town and what could be called a family friend. Last night he called to wish me a happy birthday. In calling him back and listening to the plight of Spain, the anger and disappointment he faces as a socialist who resents the changes in his party's values, I lost all the credit on the pay-as-you-go.

When the phone peeped a warning and his voice ceased, I realised with horror that I had spent 60 euros hearing how his party faithful comrades eat 'fancy shellfish', buy their children apartments and still call themselves socialists. And how the percentage of school leavers without qualifications is rising, how he and his wife work more hours for less pay, and how the morale of the people of Spain is at an all-time low. Unemployment is way up and…

I know all this. I watch the news and my friend's shop is the post office with no stamps, the tobacconist with no cigarettes.

I came to Spain on a birthday trip last week with a family group including my mother of 87. She is the only person who remembers my birthday, and every year tells of the extremely dangerous, death-defying arrival and miracle of my unscathed appearance, my coming out with a full head of dark hair, perfect skin and bright open eyes. 'Have you seen the Farquhar baby?' the doctors and nurses are alleged to have been heard saying.

My mother tells the story every year. I wonder how many more times.

Ten years ago I asked her why she had never said I was pretty. 'Women who rely on their looks age badly,' she replied unapologetically.

'She has a point,' my famously beautiful friend★ said, knowingly, when I told her.

I wonder what 'ageing well' actually means as I look at my hands covered in shiny brown scabs where once (recently) were age spots. I don't see my face, but my hands wave about in front of me and I really disliked the dark 'freckles'. I paid one hundred pounds to have them laser-zapped off by a doctor in London who said the pain was akin to hot oil being splattered on skin. It was the first time I have ever had pain described accurately.

It wasn't painful, but it was vain, and I wasn't raised to be vain.

Vanity was for the unenlightened. I said my prayers and knew that Jesus loved me. I was devout till I saw *A Clockwork Orange* at the age of 14, and then I stopped going to church. A few days ago my granddaughter suddenly announced: 'I am Mary and you are Jesus.' It came as a bit of a surprise. I had to call her mum and run down the beach to find Bethlehem. As we passed the tiny village church I said: 'Better not call me Jesus now, or I might get followed.'

She isn't being brought up in the faith, but has been living in a dream of Jesus and his birth since the school 'activity play.' She is three years old.

'Jesus is great for kids,' my friend Paul Scully★ once remarked. Oh, we laughed. My father died when he was 56.

I am at an age when people die. I have always known that.

The country witch said autumn was her favourite season; the harvest is in. I have considered the harvest, some strange fruit and not altogether what I wanted, not quite a bonny harvest festival box. Some things aren't there because they were never planted.

'Spring is overly privileged in our culture,' she said as she spoke of all the seasons and how we are the only animals who keep busy in winter under artificial light. I consider the death of winter. Electricity killed it.

In the dead of winter I know we are going to the light, whether we pop the corks or roast the chestnuts, as long as we stay alive long enough to see another spring.

My father died when he was 56.

I can't help thinking of that, this early morning. Shortly after his death I was taken to see Billy Graham by some Americans, and ran the length of a stadium to give my heart to Jesus (or Billy). I was one of the first up, and when I told my mother she looked aghast. She called me 'Billy's girl' after that. I was always teased.

My father had called me Mrs Cassius Clay on account of my love for the boxer. I loved Cassius Clay and Cliff Richard from the age of 3 and was quite shy about my feelings. I watch my beloved granddaughter being shy in similar ways and I am moved by how some things never change.

2

'Upsy daisy ducksy doe, that's the way we want to go,' chants my mother as she climbs back to our apartment. We have just come back from dinner at La Palma, a restaurant by the sea where no one goes at this time of year.

We were the only diners, and I saw the ghosts of dinners past, remembered our friend Joe★ buying a round of beers for flamenco singers there and how I'd been cross that he'd brought rock'n'roll attention to our party.

I think I was being naïve; he already had the attention. He just wanted to do something generous with it, and did. He was one of the seventies Londoners caught up with those revolutionary Spaniards of whom I wrote yesterday.

I rang my 'old one' earlier to help with a translation from today's sugar packet. A quick message – 'Can you ring back?' – cost a euro. He rang back but the ringer was off. No one heard the call.

My mother is on her way to bed, saying to herself, 'They are brave to open with no custom,' and I feel the depth of this throwaway comment.

(There were free drinks and I swallowed quite a few, so this may be a drunken episode. Number 2, as shit is sometimes known.)

I am again tapping with one thumb and wonder if my chronicles about looking both ways, ageing and change, will improve once I can type with two hands, or if this is just a (vain) hope.

I have so many messages waiting in the wings. They sit in drafts because I don't think they are good enough. They say too much or too little and are written too fast in excitable type. I am an excitable type and I want to be otherwise. I admire elegance and restraint but…

Today I was reading the wisdom on my sugar. Like fortune cookies, these messages can seem quite personal. This morning's message was about the meaning of 'goodbye' by Manuel Scorza. It reads as follows:

No sé s' sabes lo que quiere decir adiós
Adiós quiere decir ya no mirase nunca
Vivir entre otras gentes, re'rse de otras cosas,
Morirse de otras penas.

I think it translates as:

I don't know if you know what goodbye means
Goodbye means never meeting again,
Living with other people, laughing at other things,
Dying of other pains.

I don't know if it does mean that, as my Spanish is getting worse. Once it was good, but now it just sounds like it could be… but really, really isn't.

Last year I was asked to open a square in Granada. I'm still not sure why, but I did it. I spent a long time writing virtually nothing about our dead friend, whose love of Lorca, and his Spanish *novia* aroused in him a passion for Spain that I entirely understand. He was the one who bought the round at La Palma, and he wasn't so good at Spanish either. Maybe in another chapter I will include the speech I made to open Plaza Joe in Granada, but for now, I just want to say that I got help with the translation from my friend who has the post office with no stamps.

I was moved that 'lost boys' translates as '*niños eternos,*' I loved that (still do), and that 'misfits', I was told, translates as '*varios pintos*'.

I think of the word chronic. We public schoolgirls of the seventies used it as a synonym for bad, when bad never meant good, and before we realised that all words could be decoded. To say something was chronic was to reveal a certain class privilege.

My protests and tears in 1977, against the accusation of being 'a little bourgeois,' here in Spain are on my mind. As I look back at my young self, in railway workers' blue dungarees, pasting up communist party posters, I see that my then *novio* had a point.

The fact that I was so outraged was because my mother had no money, and had used my father's life insurance to send me to a 'good school'. She never owned the house in Chelsea where I grew up. She is rather proud to have lived on the 'sniff of an oil rag' (an expression I have never understood) yet unabashedly reads the *Daily Telegraph*. She is not a Tory, but says the obituaries in the *Telegraph* are 'very good, like stories'.

When I was at school the editor of the *Daily Mail* visited to speak to us girls. '*The Times*,' he said, 'is read by those who run the country, the *Guardian* by those who would like to run the country, the *Telegraph* by the aunts of those who run the country, and the *Mail*' – a pause – 'by the wives of those who run the country.'

After this he paused again, smiling out at us all. 'So,' he continued, 'I presume I am addressing my future readership.'

He was a compelling little jerk with the sort of all-purpose *bonhomie* that has always appalled me.

He sat down. I stood up.

'Thank you,' I said, 'that was funny.' And I sat down.

After that I was sent to the headmistress for a dressing-down. My insolence had been noted. It had been an honour for me to have been chosen to give the vote of thanks, and I had not only let myself down but apparently the whole school as well.

I was unrepentant. 'He got off lightly,' I told the intelligent headmistress who had dedicated her life to educating girls. She smiled a rather beautiful smile for an old woman. I think she must have been 50.

It was around this time the French teacher caught me smoking. 'Only unintelligent people smoke,' she said.

'*Au contraire*,' said I, flirtatiously tapping the back of my copy of *La Peste*, where a picture of Albert Camus made smoking look mighty fine.

I think of Camus every day, as his ability to support an idea of happiness in the midst of the bleak is inspirational. I often remember to choose the cheese sandwich. I might have it wrong, but I think he once said something about there being a choice between committing suicide and having a cheese sandwich. Or was it a cup of coffee?

Coincidentally, I have seen that the girl on the roof of the Colón in Barcelona in 1936 died on Epiphany this year. She was 94, her name was Marina Ginestà. Her obituary was in the *Telegraph* along with the photo that inspired many a little bourgeois of the 1970s.

3 *TREE*

Last night I dreamed of an old boy-friend of my sister's. He was Irish and pronounced three as 'tree.' In the dream I was looking at a greeting card which made it clear he had always loved my mother. There were kisses all over it, and declarations of a powerful passion. I remembered this man as I woke up, and was puzzled as to why he had entered my dreams along with a serious young boy fondling a showgirl.

There was a journey on a train with fluffy blue seats like water-bottle covers. The journey involved lost suitcases and mislaid tickets. It was a train to a Samuel Beckett rally taking place in a faraway stadium. Arriving on the last train with a missing ticket to 'the greatest show on earth,' I rushed about trying to find someone to listen to my plight, but I don't think I ever found anyone.

I woke and wondered about how dreams change as we age.

I think of daydreams and how nobody wishes each other 'Good daydreaming,' but they should. Or rather they could...

Recently I have been advised to remove 'should' from my vocal vulgarly, or rather my vocabulary. It is a change worth making at any age, but certainly as one pushes 60. Fuck all that punishment embedded in vocabulary.

I think of my mother staring out to sea. 'I am happy with my thoughts,' she says, but still I give her a book to read...

In the middle of decoding dreams, my friend rang. I read out the meaning of 'goodbye' by Manuel Scorza, from yesterday's sugar, and he said my translation was nearly right, but as it is clearly a farewell to *someone,* then 'you' must come into it.

Goodbye means never seeing you again

'And "dying with other *sorrows*",' he suggested, instead of 'pains'.

He remarked on my Spanish accent, saying I had always sounded sweeter and sexier in Spanish. I laughed, and imagined living here forever and dying in Spanish.

I watched someone dying in another language once, his third. At times he would cry out in his mother tongue, Hungarian, and at others in his second language, German. He cried out for what sounded like a kiss, but was in fact a cushion.

I consider death, as usual. I never knew till yesterday that Manuel Scorza had died in a plane crash in 1983. He was 55.

I think of another fatal crash. Camus died in a car accident in 1960 with the ticket, for the train he was supposed to have taken, in his pocket. He was 46.

Today I am tapping on in the spirit of come-what-may writing. This morning's sugar packet wisdom was by Seneca the Younger, giving some good advice about the importance of daring to give time to things that seem difficult or impossible. Transforming the impossible. It's unsurprising that *motivational speech* has been a feature of communication since ancient times.

I think of depression and disappointment and how many tweets give encouragement to the desperate. Always variations on a theme: 'Fail to prepare, prepare to fail.'

Yuck. Too symmetrical and reeking of Baden-Powell. I prefer ones that come out of the blue. One day I just said to myself: 'RECALIBRATE HOPE.' I didn't get it from any known source, and think it most helpful.

I've tried it on a few disappointed adults, along with the reminder to choose the cheese sandwich option, as Camus did on any given day, when the choice, between suicide or sandwich, hovered.

I mentioned 'recalibrating hope' to a friend before Christmas and he called me 'Clarence.' He said he was desperate and then I appeared and shared all the wisdom from sugar packets and beyond, and he began to recalibrate hope in front of my eyes. It's important to forget about the lost causes, but easier said than done, sometimes…

When it's tough I remember W.C. Fields, who said: 'If at first you don't succeed, try, try, try again, and then give up, don't be a damn fool about it.'

If you can't forget, then go on and remember till it's not so compelling. I think forcing forgetfulness is dangerous (at any age) but being open to the pleasure of forgetting is vital in the pursuit of recalibration.

On the subject of memory, I always quote my caustic aunt. At the time my mother was being evicted from her home of 60 years — the house in Chelsea she didn't own, my aunt was particularly tart. I will forgo telling the long and grim story, of greed in our time, so as to get to the punchline to which I am heading.

I often point out that: 'I am dedicated to a punch-line,' when I notice listeners drifting off or trying to change the subject. If I am heading somewhere particular, no matter how many detours, I always return to my path. This might be because I am a Capricorn, like Jesus, and David Bowie who, incidentally, lived in Chelsea on the same street as I did. He led a very different sort of life from mine, I presume, but always smiled at me on my way home from school. I was never able to smile back, although I practiced.

In the early seventies it was impossible to be nonchalant with David Bowie. His first girlfriend, Dana, had been to my school, so he probably liked the uniform. I knew a lot about him. He painted the inside of his house black, I heard. I don't know if it was true, but I liked the thought that his black paintwork would be white underneath, whereas our white walls were black underneath.

Our house had been a boys' crammer. A house of misery, one presumes, where little boys had to study, in what were once known as the interwar years, in black rooms.

Back to the punch-line.

My aunt, impatient with my mother's vacant stare and weepy left eye in 2003, asked me what I thought the matter was. My aunt was 90 at the time. I answered that it was a terrifying prospect to be uprooted in such a callous way at such a time, and mumbled something about the ghosts.

My aunt, in an imperious voice, asked: 'Does she believe in ghosts?' 'Well,' I said, and paused, 'memories…'

'Oh,' said the aunt, in exasperation, 'the best thing to do with memories, Marcia, is to forget them.'

I wonder about this often, while trying to remember to forget.

I look at my mother, now reading about Pompeii, and think of her staring out to sea, happy in her thoughts. I must ask her how she trains her mind to play the happy scenes over and over. I won't disturb her now, but I would like to know.

Today I received photographs from our friend in Cartagena who helped translate Scorza yesterday. His mother had escaped into France in 1936 with her little cousins, whose school-teacher parents had been brutally murdered by Franco's army. One of the cousins has written a book and we discussed it.

He said: 'You would like it, it's very personal and full of stories.'

Apparently his mother didn't want to remember or tell her story. She is my mother's age and also wants to think happy thoughts.

I remember liking his mother so much back in the seventies. She was very beautiful and very tough. We used to walk in the Retiro gardens and sometimes meet her friend, who was the daughter of Charlie Chaplin. This friend, Geraldine, asked me if I'd like to be in her husband's film about punks. Ambivalent★ as ever, I said: 'No, thank you.'

5

Recently I wrote some answers to some questions posed by an American undergraduate, a bright daughter of friends.' This was one of the questions:

Is the audience a participant in the work? Are they active/passive, and is that good/bad?

I answered from the heart, that piece of the mind that seems the most direct, and wondered afterwards whether I should have tried to sound more erudite.

The imagined professors, marking what I dubbed 'Questionnaires for unknown female artists,' loomed large but I pressed send.

This is a bit of what I wrote:

I would definitely say the audience are part of the work. They are up close, involved, engaged or otherwise, and I feel them. I see and smell them as much as they see and smell me. I wear perfume. I factor in smell. I refer to chemistry. I sometimes tell an audience that I rely on their energy for the duende. *This word, which has no translation into English, means a lot to me, as does Lorca, his life and works.*

Last year I got a mention in *El Pais* as a person to whom Joe Strummer had explained the meaning of *duende*. The journalist also gave Joe credit for having told me there was no translation into English. But I made a point of it in my square-opening speech in Granada last May. I mentioned the deceased in carefully chosen, glowing terms, and made the point about *duende* all by myself.

Lorca gave me the meaning of the term, and flamenco too, of course. My husband said it was usual for the legendary one to get the credit. Who's he telling? I have had more than my fair share of words swiped fresh out of my mouth.

How many times have I been told: 'I might use that?' I heard it not so long ago for instance when I said: 'Men are lost without the seventies.'

A certain redoubtable cosmopolitan agony aunt, doyenne of the sexual revolution, female icon to all those finding a voice to say yes (and a voice to say no), smiled as she said those same words to me.

'I might use that.'

Kind to even mention the possibility. But the implication that such borrowers could put me to better use, would know exactly what to do with my 'accidental' wisdom, gnaws at me. No such thing as an accident.

'Own your own,' I hear myself crying out. 'Time to own up, take back your words and get on with writing in your own name.'

It's what I'm doing now: essaying, trying, having a go at putting something down. It's what I always tell others. Time to do what one says.

'A little literary constipation wouldn't go amiss,' a tutor remarked when I was an undergraduate. It hurt, especially when she said I could get a job on the *Daily Express*.

Only the day before yesterday I recalled the then-editor of the *Daily Mail* visiting my school and greeting us girls as his future readers. He never even mentioned the *Express* in his classist, sexist list of British newspapers and their readership. But he might well have added: 'The *Express* is read by the cleaners of those who run the country.'

This right-wing rag, full of sensational and salacious gossip, was devoured by my bipolar aunt. The aunt who knew what best to do with memories did *not* read the *Express.*

I look back now at the gifted young academic who chastised my loose prose. She was brilliant, beautiful and loved by all the poets and writers then living in seventies London, and by a handsome husband who resembled Alfred Jarry. Her uncle was a famous explorer, and she was a socialist who lived in a marvellous house. I wondered why I couldn't be more like her; no one would ever call her a 'little bourgeois.'

I remember thinking how proud my aunt would have been had I been writing for her favourite newspaper. I winced deeply, but didn't let on.

'My aunt reads the *Express*,' I quipped as if I was in on the joke. As if it *was* a joke.

Shortly afterwards I got a more suitable tutor, whose father was a blind vicar. He understood why I favoured Beckett over Brecht.

In the early nineties I dreamed I ran to Stanley Kubrick to ask him to help a friend who had got tangled up in his garden. He was in a large and pleasant kitchen stirring a white sauce. He said he couldn't help, I said it was urgent. He stirred on, only adding, 'down with the creepy crawlies, the failed vicars' daughters go.'

 were the cigarettes the Canadian lodger smoked. Let's call him Humbert.

In the sixties I went to school with children of the beautiful people. Only one other mother, apart from mine, wore knee-length skirts. At night I would imagine my real parents; they were young Americans with big smiles and tight pants. They were Doris Day and JFK. In my prayers they would appear in a long shiny car, bursting with gifts for me, their beloved daughter, and for the kind old people who had been caring for me in their absence. The tearful, joyous reunion would end with a heartfelt promise to keep in touch with the Farquhars, and then off we'd go into the future.

My dream parents were, needless to say, very brave people who were involved in top secret work of international importance. I have always been enthralled by espionage and double-agency.

Anyway, Humbert the lodger was no Bogart. He wore the belted-up mac of a private detective but there his glamour ended.

He was in his fifties when he came to stay. He chain-smoked No.6 and I collected the cards. By cards, I suppose I mean coupons. If you collected hundreds or thousands, you could send off for gifts. Since my real parents, the Farquhars, were not in favour of material goods, I encouraged poor Humbert to smoke. When he was dying of lung cancer, ten years later, I lived in north Soho. He came on a farewell trip.

'You killed me sweetheart,' he smiled.

Poor Humbert. He was in the house when my father died. He took me to school that morning and I asked him to stand at the end of the road. I didn't want to be seen with him.

I wasn't told about my father till after school but I had thought that something was different. The headmistress, a plump aristocrat in high heels and camel-hair coat, hugged me. I smelt the gin and heady scent. My sister collected me and blurted out the shocking news as we crossed the King's Road. I screamed, and can still hear it.

My mother looked amazing that day. I see her so clearly, wearing sunglasses and a pale yellow linen suit, sitting very still in the drawing room. She was crying as she embraced me and offered me strawberries. I didn't want to eat. I only wanted to watch TV. I watched *Morph*, a shape-shifting plasticine boy. It seemed the strict rules had been abandoned that day.

I was in a trance when Humbert appeared and patted my head. I shouted: 'Go away,' and never got told off. He went.

When I returned from a month's exile in the happy family lives of others, the death was never mentioned. In this way my father just vanished. My sister said she thought she'd seen him riding a bicycle on the Embankment, but everyone silenced that one. I tried to talk about him, but my mother said: 'Time is a great healer,' and asked me to paint her a big, bright field of poppies. She had found an unwanted frame outside an art gallery and thought it needed something cheerful that would go with the carpet, which she called: 'Spanish Gold.'

She still has that painting. I look at it and think of poppies for remembrance, red poppies at the Cenotaph and the *other* poppies for forgetting. The field of poppies where Dorothy and friends fell asleep. This field is often on my mind, as are the pipes of opium I have long romanced and never smoked.

Humbert stayed on as a lodger and I punished him. He asked for it. He liked to be smacked with a ruler and I obliged. I wonder what sort of life had brought this unlikely man to Chelsea in the swinging sixties.

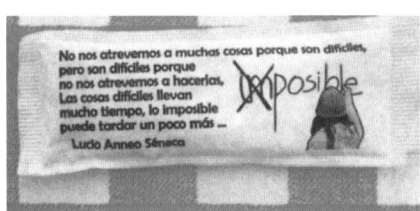

1. *Federico García Lorca*; 2. *Marina Ginesta*, Barcelona, 1936; 4. Sugar Packet; 5. Melissa Scott-Miller, *Garden at Childwickbury Manor*, 1990; 6. Marcia Farquhar, *Poppies*, 1968; 3. *Tree*, 2020.

LUCKY

7

My last episode, recalling the Canadian lodger and death of my father, unleashed a torrent of thoughts, rushing backwards. The struggle to keep up with the future, far and near, all but stopped me in my tracks.

My mother sang of a creature on a railway track, picking its teeth with a carpet tack, on her way to the bathroom on our last night in Spain. 'Polly Wolly Doodle, all the day… Fare thee well.'

I think my mother chooses good songs quite accidentally. She is ready for the journey home hours in advance and enters an almost trance-like state. We go up into the night sky and see the moon together. Our future holds the final farewell or, as my mother calls it, 'the single ticket.'

A notoriously drug-addled friend of my age says he has promised his mother that he will outlive her. I understand this and hope he does. I hope I do, but dread it too. I hate goodbyes. I have often said so.

'Best part of any visit,' once quipped a ready wit, and made me laugh. It now makes me ruminate, without a smile.

I haven't got over the sixties. I was there and so was my father, and then he wasn't. Often called 'real,' I realise I don't feel real. I often say this out loud.

Back in London I get stuck. I whistle 'Polly Wolly Doodle, all the day' and protest too much that 'I don't give a fuck.' But I am in a jam and onwards is a revolving door. I think of Janus as the god of doorways, and the door that's both open and shut.

Getting on and *passing through*…

'Getting on' is a good phrase. I seize on all the meanings. Ageing, of course; persevering; and being at ease with another. I am, and am not, getting on.

And 'passing through', which hits me in the deep anatomy. We are all passing through, however stuck, so I tell myself.

I go and see a homeopath and am given remedies for grief. I lose them, and after a late night search that involves my husband, they are nowhere. It's typical, I think, and remember to try to avoid reiterating the negative. He says they'll turn up in the morning, and only then do I relax and notice I am sitting on them. He has long maintained that I have always been sitting on everything I've ever been looking for, and he has a point.

I take the tiny sugar ball and hope it does the trick.

'It's only a trick,' say the doctors of rationality. And so what if it is? Surely it's just a matter of playing good-enough tricks.

'It's not easy being anyone,' I say to my brother, who has often mistaken me for Riley, the one whose life is famously easy.

'When did you last see your father?' was once a euphemistic enquiry as to bowel movements. My brother last saw our father on my seventh birthday. We were on a railway station. I had been given a ten bob note and went to buy my brother butterscotch. I remember it cost two shillings out of the ten I had been given. I came back to the family. My father smacked me for going missing, my mother said something about the kindness of my thought. My brother kissed my mother, said: 'Goodbye, little fellah,' to me, and our father said something about high waves in the Cape of Good Hope and a wish for them to never meet again. My brother walked away without looking back. He never took the butterscotch, and father and son never did meet again.

'I hope *you* die in a wave,' I said out loud, under my breath. My father laughed. 'You won't forget this birthday, 7 on the 7th,' he said. 'I will,' I said.

INFIN **8**

I lie in bed, seeing 8 on its side looking like infinity, and remember first drawing 8, one circle on top of another.

My granddaughter's name begins with O.

She asked me, when she first realised this: 'What is the O for Marcia?' Indeed.

She draws circles freely and regularly. I learned to draw a circle last weekend. With a brush full of black ink, I waited for the moment and exhaled. It was perfect. Maybe not Giotto-perfect but bright, black and alive.

I want to paint circles, not go round in them.

Back to the fresh start earlier today. It was 8.15. I thought of the chocolate and mint cream squares called 'After Eight', which I once believed to be the height of sophistication. Imre★ used to offer them with a cunning smile. 'It is always after eight,' he would say, suggestively.

I never quite got it. I did understand the same look and tone when he'd give my friends his phone number with an emphasis on the 69. 'Riverside *69* double-O.' This was quite embarrassing when we were 19 and he was pushing 80.

I think of him and me at tea after seeing Leonardo's anatomical drawings at the Royal Academy in the seventies. He had paid for my ticket and bought me a catalogue, so I wanted to pay for the tea. I went to the till, took out my purse and was intercepted in an impatient manner. I mentioned the exhibition, the catalogue, my pleasure until, in a very loud voice, he shouted:

'I AM NOT A GIGOLO.'

The Piccadilly tea set tittered, some even laughed out loud.

'I don't think anyone would think I had paid to be with you,' I retorted, loudly enough to entertain strangers in a tea room.

I didn't add: 'Especially as I am sixty years younger and five inches taller than you.'

Recently a bodybuilder wrote to me from Fort Myers, Florida, to say he had a painting of my father, Imre Goth. And even more recently, I heard from an author who was wondering about writing a biography about my father. He also wanted information. I only told them that Imre Goth was not my father.

Maybe I'll write about disinclination to engage in biographies at another point, but this morning's hour of writing about eight, and smiling back at Imre, got interrupted by an email entitled 'not very good news' and left me shouting 'fuck' again.

9

'Everyone of them knew that as time went by they'd get a little bit older and a little bit slower but…' John never did.

Lennon and Farquhar were two Johns who never did get old.

I called my father 'John.' He didn't like names like Daddy or Pop. He loved *A Spaniard in the Works*. He said: 'You have to know how to spell' when we read it together and I didn't laugh. He had teeth like a vampire and a laugh like a snake. His voice was beautiful. When I first heard John Cale reciting the sad ballad of Waldo Jeffers, I listened again and again. I couldn't stop. My brother said it was because he sounded like 'our' John.

My brother cut up an onion on hearing the news of John Farquhar's death in July 1967, but remained tearless. He said he had wanted to look sad-eyed for a party but the onion didn't work. He was just 21, a cub reporter on the *Rand Daily Mail* in South Africa, and I was a misfit little Chelsea girl of 9.

'He checked in as a lodger and checked out as a stiff,' remarked my brother on our father's association with the house in O Street. It's true he had arrived in uniform (Fleet Air Arm) to find a room in a bohemian part of town. He was bored at Brown's.★

Twice court-martialled in the war, the first time for smashing the controls of a plane he deemed unfit for flight, and then, having been missed (he was apparently a great pilot and a great dancer), he was taken back, only to be expelled again for pissing in front of dignitaries in Trinidad.

'I thought I was in a urinal,' he said in his defence.

I loved my John and could see he was troubled. I once drew him with a turned down mouth. 'Can't you give me a smile?' he asked.

'Not till you give me one,' I said.

He told me about Jiddu Krishnamurti, saying that he liked Krishnamurti because he had said he wasn't a deity. I didn't really get why someone saying they weren't a god was so praiseworthy. He explained that many people had brought him over from India as a boy and elected him a deity but he had refused the mantle.

He told me about Gandhi and the horrors of the world.

I can see why he loved John Lennon, Mahatma Gandhi, Alan Turing, Martin Luther King, Karl Marx, Carl Jung and Albert Einstein… but Ken Dodd?

The year he died was the year that *Sergeant Pepper* came out. After the final session at the studio, The Beatles came to play the acetates at the house where Mama Cass was staying, at the other end (later, the Bowie end) of my street.

According to my friend Darryl,★ neighbours applauded and shouted 'Louder, louder!' and so the speakers were turned out to face the street in the middle of that first night.

I didn't hear any of this but like to imagine it coincided with my father checking out, newspaper taxi waiting to take him away to join the atoms.

X

I like Roman numbers, especially ten.

X looks like a letter for voting, kissing and seeing through (X-ray vision).

'On my 4th birthday, I'm going to be 10,' says O for Olive, and I laugh because she is serious and because choosing what age to be makes me wonder. I think and can't think of being any other age.

This is the age for me, this is my day. Ahem…

This isn't a diary, but present time, whereabouts and company do impact. Well, I am in Snape in Suffolk. I am keeping quiet about *Pushing 60*. There are great writers here. I drank a lot last night and blurted out a lot of unnecessary information, but never mentioned the iPhone novella.

I have decided that all 60 chapters will be thumbed. I have a flexible, double-jointed thumb. The precision of its darting sideways action is regularly impressive but the compelling obscenities and absurdities that sometimes burst out are even better, instant joys (Joyce).

Thumbs up for vocal vulgarly (vocabulary) in my third chapter, the one called *Tree*.

Looking forward is not always fun. I've spent a dark dawn looking forward in fear at the things I have to do, such as passing on the 'not very good news' to my mother. She left me a message last night: 'You're a great little cricket,' she said. I pressed to save (for a week).

What a wonderful night last night was. Patrick Keiller showed me his concessionary travel card. He corrected me when I called it a 'Freedom pass.' I wonder if I'll ever get a Freedom pass, or its equivalent. All my generation are getting these tickets to ride, or looking forward to them, but now there is talk of putting a stop to it all. Imagine wanting to put a stop to us lot getting something for nothing and travelling about causing trouble.

'No future,' sang another John, long long ago. And here we are. The Silver Jubilee was over 35 years ago.

The other day I was having my hair cut and tossed. It looked like flaxen candyfloss for 15 minutes but lost its airy bounce on the way to the Hayward. (Is it true that Thatcher's research at Oxford revolved around how much air could be pumped into ice cream before it collapsed?)

As my hair was filling with hot air, I saw a familiar face at the window. It was none other than my friend Shanne Bradley, who I haven't seen for years. Her old band, The Nipple Erectors, is still a favourite on my playlist.

She came in and we talked of dead and dying punk-time people, and the living, of course. I asked her what had happened to Helen, who was known as Helen of Troy back in the day, when she accompanied Malcolm McLaren. Helen was very fond of him, said he listened to sentimental songs with tears in his eyes, information which somehow made me loathe him all the more.

She, Helen, was initially my brother's friend from South Africa in the far-out sixties. She told me she had been put on a worldwide registry of eligible Jewish dwarves because her father had wanted her to find a suitable boy. She escaped the paternal plan by following my brother back to London and going to Goldsmiths.

My mother and I were in the canteen at Goldsmiths, waiting to see my brother play Oberon, when I first saw Helen.

'Is Duncan's friend a…?'

'Would you like a KitKat, Marcia?'

My mother, who never offered much in the way of chocolate, intercepted so quickly that I realised she was uncomfortable with where my question was going.

My brother was painted SILVER, and I think he was totally naked, but whether he had a metallic fig-leaf or not, he was nude enough for my mother and me to feel awkward. We were not avant-garde then, or even bohemian.

Helen remembers my mother's beauty and strength, which she puts down to being a Taurus woman like herself. I don't know why I have given Helen's memories in the present tense. I haven't seen her since the GOLDEN Jubilee, when some of us, including Shanne, watched fireworks from Parliament Hill. And then Helen vanished.

'She wasn't at her friend Malcolm's funeral, so I heard from Sophie,'★ I rattle on with a mouthful of hairspray.

Shanne said she'd heard that Helen had gone to Canada.

'Oh yes, that's where she has a sister who's a surgeon. My brother lives there too...' When he went missing (for years from '71 on) Helen would talk about him...

My brother, before he disappeared, wore safety pins and razor blades on military ribbons and asked the barber to give him a Napoleon. This was not a known cut. He was no hippy, my brother. I think my brother's sartorial aberrations had an impact on the look of punk. I muse on unknown muses.

I once asked my mother if she thought she had been Imre's muse. 'Oh yes,' she answered, 'he found me amusing.'

COMING **11** BACK TO
PUSHING 60
AFTER FOUR YEARS

At last we have a number on our door, after twenty years… 'It looks like a pause,' observed Richard Dudanski.★

Haven't quite worked out what to do with proper nouns or names yet. Maybe footnotes or aliases. Snake Hips Dudanski is already an alias, a name given at a point other than the date of arrival. A name for a young adult that stuck.

Anyway, he said the slightly rounded number ones, side by side on the front of our house, look like a pause symbol.

I like the fact that the eleven looks like a pause and, coming back after nearly four years to *Pushing 60*, I resume on eleven, a pause.

A pause is a good place to start again. There is silence in a pause and I hope to make more of silence.

I often recall Lis Rhodes, the filmmaker and my one-time tutor, asking me why I spoke so fast and how she helped me to pause. I asked Lis if she considered speed and volume in the female voice to be a feminist issue, and she said that she did.

It wasn't for nothing the Saatchi brothers advised Thatcher to correct her voice. That voice, of slow deliberation in lowered tones, was clever. I have noticed that the more powerful the person, the quieter the voice. Those who know others will make the effort to listen, speak softly.

I spoke loudly as a child, living with a deaf grandmother.

No more shouting for me. It's time for the quiet voice, the still small voice. Silence and space.

The number eleven on the door was spray-painted through a stencil that arrived ready-made in the stiff card around which a new shirt was folded. Credit where it's due, Jem saw the stencil and I shook the can. It all ran down, dribbly, and we laughed.

I hadn't read the instructions. It's important to shake for minutes, not seconds.

He redid it beautifully and painted periwinkle blue around the new, hard edged silver shapes.

The date 11/11 is Remembrance or Poppy Day. I have been reading out my long-ago writings from January 2014, so am reminded of my double understanding of the symbolism of poppies. This backwards and forwards of *Pushing 60's* musings is, in many ways, an exercise in remembering and forgetting.

I often say I have been living with the dead all my life, but actually I think that is an exaggeration. I have been living with them, or him, for 50 years. Trying to remember, and forget.

Reading back, I think of David Bowie saying hello on Oakley Street like a shy boy, when he was Ziggy. He was good as a shy boy, better at it than the real boys who affected cool but were just nowhere near the real McCoy.

I did smile, I remember now, but an awkward smile because I was caught between innocence and experience in all the wrong ways.

My friend, who did smile back with the grand confidence of a shire beauty, and did accept an invitation, said he was boring. Just like all those boys who wanted to be him. She was truly nonchalant, ended up marrying a prince. I saw her once again in Battersea Park, with a child named after an empire, Otto for short.

I saw *him* once again, in the eighties, at a gig. He smiled again, that same smile, and I hid behind a pillar at the Hammersmith Palais. It must have seemed rude but I was a real shy girl. The next day a tabloid paper announced David Bowie was going to join the Pogues. I cut it out and put it on our notice board, just another lie in newsprint.

My brother said he was driving when he heard that Bowie had died, and he said he knew he had died for him. Jesus Christ. My brother and so many others. I didn't think anything of the sort but looked up Oakley Street and David Bowie. And found out that his house had been a hive of goings-on at the time of my encounters with the boy up the road.

Once in the seventies I went on my own to Senate House to hear an Indian poet.

I was transported by the chanting rhythms and thrilled by the beauty of the poet. After an hour or so my mind was wandering back to Soho. I was ready for other sorts of poetry; quite suddenly the spell was broken, I couldn't bear to listen to any more. I wanted to escape. I caught the eye of a girl on a similar wavelength.

I cannot remember if the recitation came to an end or we left, but I do remember liking her and us finding our own fun. She hoped we would meet again. Me too. She said she was very relieved to meet someone of her own age, who was not just a fan of her brother.

'I might be, but I don't know who your brother is,' said I. She demurred, and after a while said: 'David Bowie.'

'Oh,' I said, 'this might prove difficult because I prefer him to you.'

I wasn't sure if I was joking. She looked hurt so I said I, too, was somebody's sister. Well, a somebody/nobody's sister.

I spoke of my brother so as to avoid her having to speak of hers. We parted and I never did see her again. When her brother died I looked up the family, but there was no mention of a sister.

11/11 is also the day of celebration of corduroy, *Hail the Wail*. The wail being the raised fat bit of the material, I believe.

I remember Paul Neagu visiting the Slade and talking to me. I was working with fur and we discussed the ethics of materials. He added corduroy to the list of contentious materials and I shrieked: 'CORDUROY?!' What could *possibly* be immoral about this most innocent of fabrics?

But he hadn't said corduroy, he had said *cod roe*.

When I went to Edinburgh earlier in the summer, to interview Richard Demarco★ for *Vox Box*,★ he told me that Paul Neagu was one of the greatest artists who had ever lived. I said I remembered him well.

I remember the dead, but while there is life, I had best return to *now*.

This isn't a topical daily, but I cannot help hearing my own shriek among the many women and men who have bravely lambasted the violators, those who abused them *because they could.* Easy to be silenced by shame and fear. Not all silence is good.

When I was eleven, a red-haired man cornered me in a shopfront in Ballymena, Antrim, and exposed himself. I saw a very pale penis. I wonder if I have imagined the freckles. I shook and shook and my dear friend embraced me and cried.

Her father made no complaint because I was an English girl and it was at the time of the Troubles (so called). Post-truth has a long history.

I just remembered that the same friend was in Italy when I was raped after getting into a car in a scenario that seemed so safe. A ride for two of us, but the car door swung shut on me. I can still see his teeth.

She embraced me again when I returned, in a sort of euphoria of being alive. I had put up a fight and then, in the middle of nowhere-I-knew, in a car, I played nice because I wanted to live.

I will never forget his little teeth.

My mother still lives. She is between worlds, sometimes enjoying the attention of Éamon de Valera, who is always ready to throw back his head and roar with laughter at her joke (just the one), but at other times she is plagued by the man who tried to rape her when she was a girl.

She believed he wanted to see the walnut trees. She was told to take him to see them and, as she presented the beautiful trees, he laughed and said: 'Do you really think I have come to see walnut trees?'

No complaint could be made; her father owed him money. My mother is ripped apart each time that dark scene plays, and I would go into her head and kill him with my bare hands if I only could. I dream of ripping off his head and vomiting down his neck.

I wake and ask if this is something I might have seen in a real movie. Nobody knows, but I get a few looks for having asked.

'Tell me what you said to Éamon de Valera,'★ I say, to switch reels.

She answers: 'I said to him "so you could say you are a Spanish onion in an Irish stew" to which he roared out laughing, threw back his head and *roared.*'

WOMAN- 12 HOOD AND THE HANGED MAN

All our days are measured in two periods of twelve hours. Noon and midnight are beautiful everyday words that go with twelve.

I think about twelve. Twelve months of the year, twelve Olympian gods, twelve apostles, twelve signs of the zodiac and twelve stars on the European flag.

I love Banksy's mural at Dover, in which a British worker, up a ladder in overalls and flat cap, grimly chisels away a star — the UK star — out of the European constellation.

But of course: 'Their number shall be invariably set to twelve, the symbol of completeness and perfection.'

A year or so ago, I altered some playing cards into a tarot pack of sorts: images, events and notes associated with the life of Austin Osman Spare. I learned more about tarot in doing so, and was particularly drawn to the hanged man, number 12 in the Major Arcana. He represents being at a crossroads, self-sacrifice, meditation and letting go. Yes to all that, a good card. I took it, and take it, personally.

Living in suspension, surrendering and letting go of control, being a willing victim to topsy-turvydom, accepting indecision…

I look at my mother and I hear from my other-than-conscious mind, 'Hold dear and let go.' I look at the body from whence I came and think of 'womanhood', as she always called it. When does it start? And when and where does it end? My mother's timetable was always linked to the coming and going of blood.

As women age, they are often asked about the onset of menses and their cessation. My mother cheered me through the menopause: 'You won't know yourself.' Always a positive in her book of tributes to the future, but unnerving for me, who was always hoping I *would* know myself.

I drift back to my first-blooded pyjamas.

It was holiday time so my mother's friend said she would take me to a dog show. I don't have a single memory of that day apart from walking in on her brother, mid-bowel movement.

My mother's friend was kind, big, with hands like a man. Bert Lahr★ in drag; she looked like her spaniels. Maybe on purpose. Her hair was bottle-cocker and she punctuated comments of no great impact with 'Boom Boom'.

She was what was called an heiress. She was also what was called highly strung. There was a brother who looked like a soft white boulder. Much good all that shipping wealth had done poor Hardy. He wasn't quite right. He came to Olympia and held hands with his sister. At some point I walked in on him and he looked mildly back at me, maybe thought I'd come to help. I liked this giant baby man. He was very gentle and it's odd to think that I was with him the day I bled my way to womanhood.

My mother, who had discovered the evidence, wanted me to know. She had rung to ask how I was and had been told that I appeared not to have seen or noticed anything. I assume they agreed I could bleed on in ignorance. Boom Boom.

When I got home there was a little ceremony.

'Welcome to womanhood,' said my mother, who had a belt and a packet of Dr White's looped sanitary towels.

What is the definition of innocence? Answer: the boy in the Dr White's factory, thinking he's making hammocks for mice. That was a joke we told back then.

My mother and sister wondered if they should stay at home with the new woman, but decided it wasn't necessary and wished me a good night. Later, their laughter woke me. They were laughing out loud at the used sanitary towel and belt left neatly on my bedside table.

'It's a 24-hour day!' hooted my sister, and they exchanged those looks that would probably now be filed under the word *bless*.

I'm writing this now beside my sleeping mother. A voice calls out in broken

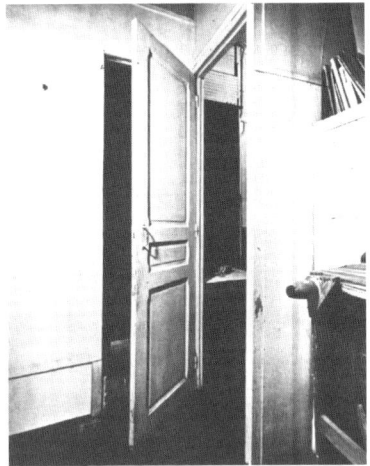

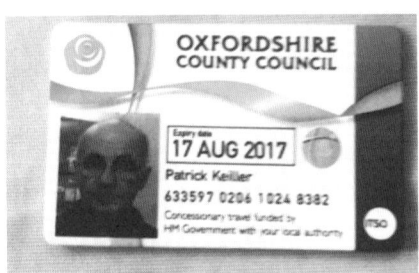

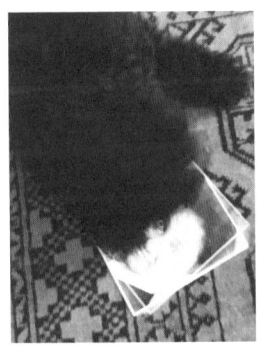

7. Marcel Duchamp's open and shut door, 11 rue Larrey; 8. Photograph of a *Self Portrait of Imre Goth* bought by a body builder in Fort Myers, Florida, 2014; 12. Tarot cards made by Marcia Farquhar; 11. *Pause*; 9. Ken Dodd; 10. *Pass*.

English 'I think she pass away,' and another answers: 'Wait, I'm coming.' Dishes on a distant trolley sound like radio play effects, as do an old lady's groans. The crying out loud persists, the distant television news carries on, and a human cry, on the cat spectrum, cuts in. There is no sound from the room of the dead. The room next door that is. It is quiet. My mother's breathing is gentle.

I change the water in some flowers and remember the breath of a dentist. I once joked he had the breath of a corpse.

13

A bingo-call truth. Not unlucky for intellectuals and occultists.

The thirteenth plate comes to mind, the plate that never was, and how its absence was the cause of so much outrage and pain. The missing plate and invitation was all it took to change a good fairy into an evil fury. I can relate to that, and being pricked.

So many stories full of needles and lost years, spinning wheels of fortune and thickets. I see my younger self, journeying through the thickets and sleeping through life.

'Wake up, Marsha!' the trainer shouted at me in the EST⋆ training. I was 21 and fast asleep. 'Do you mean me?'

There was a famous pop star, whose name I forget, who catcalled when I went up on stage for my correction. That's when I got: 'Wake up, Marsha.'

The famous person didn't come to the end-of-training party, but his manager did, and said it had changed his life.

The other participant who didn't come was one of the great train robbers. He too had seen the light.

Only I had not, probably because I was asleep.

The others who didn't turn up for the reveal – *the secret is that there is no secret* eureka moment – were the casualties who had rocked and wept and been taken out. I hope they got their money back. I tried to get mine back, which wasn't mine but Alan's, the good lodger who dignified my confusion with conversations about death and madness. He, who understood queer silence and knew melancholy, and was my friend.⋆

'Does it get better?' I asked him, when I was a very young girl. 'No, worse,' he said, in a terse Welsh way.

Later, when he was 70, he phoned me to apologise for that depressing reply decades ago, and to report from the bright side that it does get better. He was happy at last, gay and out.

I look at his young face, in an old painting from the fifties, that hangs in my mother's room as she sleeps.

I watch my mother and listen to the bed. She is a sleeping hawk. I see why my father called her Horatio. I look from the portrait of young Alan to the Kerry Hills, her favourite painting, a watercolour that she has been protecting from a harpy who rushes in after dark to paint in a lake that never was, that never was there.

A month ago, I foolishly said I remembered there had always been a lake. This was a big mistake and upset my mother, who looked furiously at me and coldly announced that she would have to call the artist. Only the artist could confirm that there had never been a lake, and I should ask the artist himself if I didn't believe her.

The frightening art vandal also comes to apply what my mother calls 'Red Indian feathers' to a painting of my brother, aged 8. He cries out for her to leave him alone, but she only rams the feathers on his head more fiercely, as my mother shouts for the police.

I think of Imre, lying in the cancer ward in Charing Cross Hospital, wearing a dressing up box headdress of coloured feathers, applied to his head by an insane socialite who made whoops around the bed and offered to be his squaw. He called me back and asked me to remove the feathers and get him out of the hospital, and home, before they could steal all his paintings.

'Nobody is going to do that,' I said. But actually, they did.

The morning after his death, the cancer ward squaw sent her groom and horse box to his studio. Imre's Hungarian next of kin were sent proceeds from the sale of the studio, but no paintings. Those powerful, thieving country lifers, in league with the last mistress, *swiped the lot,* to borrow from my mother's vocabulary…

They put them up for sale through Sotheby's. That's how come the bodybuilder in Fort Myers, Florida, had a little collection, and Barbra Streisand too, I hear.

My mother has beautiful fingers, locked now into twisted shapes. I compare the back of our hands. Mine, which look so scrawny and claw-like when alone, seem well padded beside the hands that could not be thinner. I look at the age spots, all but covering her hands, and think back to 2014 when I had my own removed.

They have come back and I am fine with them now. I am getting used to the *new age* spots (ho ho).

To know something well is to know it like the back of your hand, so when such a place becomes unfamiliar, it is a shock.

In this case the shock of the new is old. Ugliness is just something unfamiliar. Draw anything and it isn't ugly anymore. I draw, and am drawn to, motley things.

I dream that I am woken by the sound of huge sheets of processed cheese lying in tatters on the bedroom floor, being decimated by retching Bonzo and rats who dart backwards and forwards. I shoo them away but they scare me. There is other filth on the floor of the room where Jem,★ Kathy B★ and I are up on the bed. I begin to clear up the cheese, lifting the big wet sheets and wrapping other rubbish into them.

Earlier we have walked across a stepped wooden structure. I am advised not to look down into the stinking sludge between the slats, because not only is it vile to see and to smell, but it is also where disgusting acts are committed by VIPs and politicians.

Waiting for a plane to take off, I am invited to a better class of seat, but it doesn't appeal. Too many screens, children and potted plants. I go back to a seat at the very back, which seems almost disconnected from the body of the aircraft. I am much happier.

I never would sit in seat 13 on a plane. I was cured of my extreme fear of flying by being told that Ronald Reagan also used to believe that his constant state of fearful mental vigilance kept the plane up.

I mentioned this to a friend, who is a comedian★ and also a recovering flight-phobe, and added that I still knew many who were terrified. He said he was relieved.

'It's reassuring to know *someone* is keeping it up,' he said, in Omagh deadpan.

14

Dreamed of my mother's funeral and how sad I was to have missed the Communion. Kitty kept me a wafer and said they were faulty; took at least five minutes to dissolve.

It had all happened very quickly, apparently. When I arrived, people asked where the body was, but I didn't know, which was true. And then I saw a little hand, with a dark red jewel flanked by diamonds, and took it from under a cloth. I saw eyes open in deep red sunken sockets.

'Oh, it's you again,' said the exhausted voice with resignation, and I hoped these were not going to be the last words my mother ever spoke to me.

On waking, I remembered my old fear of being buried alive, how close life and death can seem. There is no such thing as a living corpse.

I remind myself. Re-*mind* myself. Come into morning, mind, and bat away the nightmares.

'You fear zombies, so what? You are not alone.' I decode the everlasting wafer and fears of the undead.

Recently I put a ring on my mother's hand that she gave me when I was 40.

'They are our birth stones,' she told me, back then in 1998. Hers, diamond, and mine, garnet. The tiny flashes of diamond flank the dark red garnet, a semi-precious gemstone, as good as a ruby to me.

There is a bit more to the dream that I hold back.

I once lent, but never saw again, a medicine cabinet. It went to the Wellcome and I wrote an essay on decoding its contents. The straight-talking pills and ointments of orthodox medicine tell of sore tails and other body parts, and are confession enough, but nothing compared to the heretical remedies revealing, as they do, hidden anxieties, trauma and discoloured emissions.

Innocent dream-talk spills secrets and beans. Now I have the opportunity to write words down, and to think before I speak, there is a censor swinging over my tapping and I cannot finish the dream, except to say we seemed to be nowhere.

Nowhere is now *here*, where I am now. Ahem.

I think back to a real scene, when I was 14 and thought my mother had died. She was quite herself one minute, and the next thrown back as if by a great force landing on her bed. I can't remember why I was in her bed, but I was.

It was early one morning and she was just getting up. I called her name but she was gone, her eyes rolled back in her head and her stiff arms crossed over her chest. It was a classic death pose. I ran up to my brother and said: 'She's dead.'

He came down with me and agreed it looked like death. My sister, the nurse, appeared minutes later, woken by my howling. She was impatient with the hysterics and yet I remember she wasn't so sure of the state of our mother herself, because she called an ambulance and the family doctor, who prescribed Librium for me.

My mother was taken off on a stretcher, and I sobbed my heart out.

My brother's friend, once a monk and also, coincidentally, once a bottom in Yoko Ono's film,★ was also in the house that morning. He was called Sivers, but that morning I renamed him Shivers. He was enjoying the drama rather too much for my liking.

No idea how much more of the morning passed, but I do remember I was on my way to St Stephen's★ to find out for myself, as no word had come, when an ambulance drew up outside the house and my mother stepped out, holding an empty tin foil pudding bowl. She greeted me breezily. My sister assisted the homecoming in a professional manner, and nobody quite knew what had happened.

I loved the Librium and remember putting on my acid yellow crepe frock with bilberries on it (the Ossie Clark dress, given to me by the prostitute next door) and going out to tea with boys. I had never felt so happy; my mother was alive and I was in the best dress and dream ever.

What happened that day was never given a name. Someone said the same thing had happened to Mrs MacNair and she was stopped from riding her bicycle. My mother called it a dress rehearsal.

I asked for more Librium when I heard that the doctor said he had been most concerned about me that day. I thought I might get a lifelong supply, but my mother said it wasn't good for me. She threw away my remaining pills and some weed of my brother's. She said she did not wish to live among drug addicts and time wasters.

She lived on a farm when she was a girl, and told me that I was the sort of girl she would have called a *silly lily*.

I have a picture of her at this age, which I look at deeply and intently. She is indeed very lovely.

Around this time, talent scouts appeared at the farm looking for her because she had appeared in a production at The Abbey in Dublin. One of her sisters was a student there and had recruited my reluctant mother, who got an ecstatic mention in the *Irish Times*.

'I never wanted to be an actress,' said my mother, 'and when the talent scouts arrived saying they were looking for me, I hid.'

My mother, telling this story recently, said, that when the entertainment industry gentlemen announced: 'We have come to find a very talented young girl.' She replied: 'You won't find me here.'

She remembers how she was taken to London and cried all night. Her mother showed no mercy. She was taken to Elstree and put in make-up. A girl brought out some tweezers.

'Please do not pluck me. I live on a farm, I am not a silly lily.'

When asked to sell flowers in a cockney accent for a screen-test, she said she didn't know what it was, so they instructed her: '*Flarhs, lahv-erly flahrs*'.

Her mother was told that they could make her daughter a star, if she returned in two years time. The daughter only wanted to go back to Ireland and become a nurse.

Recently my mother asked me to pay back a debt to Miss Aherne, the school teacher who had never been paid by her parents. I said it was already sorted. Miss

Aherne had offered my mother to stay and be trained as the village school teacher. My mother said recently she was sorry she hadn't taken up the offer.

I said: 'Well I'm glad you didn't, or I wouldn't be here.' 'Really?' she said, and closed her eyes.

She is more there than here now. Thinks she sleeps in her parents' room, and sure that Éamon de Valera is asking her to marry him, but that she cannot accept, as she is old enough to be his mother.

She often tells me how they met at a reception in London in the fifties and how she remarked on his Spanish name and asked if he had Spanish blood. My mother tells me once again how de Valera said he did indeed have Spanish ancestry, causing her to make her famous joke, 'so you could say you are a Spanish onion in an Irish stew.'

The hostess of the evening was apparently not pleased with my mother.

'Oh,' said my mother, 'she was wearing a green dress. Green for Ireland, you know, and green for the other.'

At this, a knowing look implies *the other* is envy, as my mother adds: 'She was not at all pleased that I had made him laugh. He threw back his head and he roared out laughing.'

I can imagine my mother, in her late twenties, charming the honoured guest, who would have been in his seventies by this time.

He visits quite often but I always miss him. He is very keen on the marriage and cannot believe my mother is so much older than he. I say that I don't think age is an impediment.

'Do you not?' asks my mother.

I never mention anything else regarding matters of the quick and the dead.

The day-before-yesterday's dream, in which I preferred the back seat in the plane, away from the potted plants, children and screens, comes back. I think I want to be up at the front in the good seats, but I am happy at the back, in a seat which is almost disconnected from the aircraft.

I think of Cathy on the moors, and that beautiful phrase from *Wuthering Heights* – 'Heaven did not seem to be my home.'

15

My fleshy jawline is being squeezed. Or, as it turns out, my whole face is being gripped and twisted. A hand turns into a clamp and rotates my face off. I see things and know I am conscious. I'm back in the game and being warned not to look at the singer again, as I know what happened last time.

I haven't a clue what happened last time, but I seem to belong in this very dirty carnival, where my face is being squeezed off.

Pink vodka melon cocktails are being served on a tray. A little old woman is drinking them greedily but suddenly, without warning, she is outed as an imposter and chased away.

The woman on stage says everything is boring. She shows a model town in a box and slices through it, saying again: 'It's boring.'

I want to ask her for a synonym. She passes me after the show and so I do ask for a synonym, and that is when I get my face squeezed off as a punishment.

Her partner, a villainous vaudevillian with one beady and one shrivelled eye, attacks me for having been rude and I don't care. I go on about the word *boring* and defend my right to ask for a synonym, and then my face is squeezed off again.

I don't know if it keeps growing back, because I'm awake now.

This hasn't been a dream about losing face, but of having had it ripped off, stolen. They steal my face because I ask for a synonym for boring.

Stop thieves. Who are they, in the ghost train of selves?

I am happy at least that in the dream *I* challenged the vicious party-doll nihilists of the night.

Having been through my dreams with a German psychoanalyst from the age of 28 to 40, I have a dozen years of antidote to apply to the wounds of superstitious dream interpretation, received in the womb, and afterwards, through the missing breast milk. But still, I have to remember to stand up for the rational on those occasions when it is the better option.

My mother always had an ear for the banshee, was prone to announce a death with great certainty after dreaming of being in her childhood home.

Yet, she is more *there* than here now, asleep in her parents' room. Sometimes she tells me about her friends on the farm, as if they are all still there, going about their business.

'Somewhere over a rainbow.' I begin to hum tunelessly.

She tells me King's face has grown back, and how he came to say he was alive and well. I greet the news with relief, and say how much I would have liked to have met him.

'Have you not?' she asks.

This is the first I've heard of his face. I am among spooks again. I know he was killed in a terrible accident after leaving to work somewhere else, but nothing more detailed. There are many stories of his kindness to my mother which she has often told. But this mention of his beautiful face growing back, after my own peculiar dream, *puts the heart across me*, so to speak, in my mother's mother tongue.

I am not sorry when she moves on to the debt which is always on her mind.

Again, she asks me to pay the school teacher. She tells me again how ashamed she is that Miss Aherne was never paid, and how all the other children had their envelopes. I tell her it is already sorted. Again.

16

Time passes and I think of the regret of yesterday. My mother was always a battle-axe when it came to self-pity and would have none of it.

I think back to the time when I first started *Pushing 60* in 2014, and how she was sitting, looking out to sea, replaying happy reels.

I try playing a few old reels myself, *Happy Days,* and think of Winnie.

I loved *Not I*, *Krapp's Last Tape*, and *Endgame,* which I saw at the Royal Court in 1973,⋆ when I worked in a chemist on the King's Road and spent my wages on taking myself to the theatre. I like that I did that, am pleased to go back and chance upon a young self who didn't just wait to be taken.

I didn't see *Happy Days* when it was on a couple of years later. My mother did. She'd been taken to see it by an elderly couple on a visit to London, because Peggy Ashcroft was in it and it was on at the National, but they didn't like it and left. My mother told me she'd said: 'If you don't mind, I'm loving it,' and she had stayed for the Q and A afterwards.

I asked her to read it aloud, and she did, and it made sense, the giving meaning to meaninglessness, the courage of keeping going.

The very stuff of my girlish mockery of my own middle-aged mother's relentless cheerfulness was revealed that morning as something valiant and, of course, absurd.

'I am up to my waist now, Marcia,' she had said that morning, when I marvelled at her brilliance. Now she is up to her neck, a head in a bed, and I am in it beyond the waist.

There is much future behind me and nearly all of it's behind her. I contemplate the rituals of keeping going and brush my hair.

It's being so cheerful that keeps me going. She knew…

I never mentioned the number 15 in my last episode because I got waylaid by a dream of having my face squeezed off, and the curious coincidence of being told of someone else whose face had miraculously grown back. But I was 15 when I worked in the chemist's on Saturdays. It was unusual for anyone from my school to be in London at the weekend, let alone working in retail.

But there I was.

I told my mother about the manager's wandering hands and she said he'd been taken at Tobruk so was not to be blamed for his proclivities. And besides, 'Jobs are hard to get'. She always made excuses for men from the war.

The Spanking Colonel of Chelsea was a laughing stock, but my mother said something about prisoner of war camps and silenced any mirth with truly ghastly stories of torture. The colonel paid girls to spank him, or was it the other way round…

Anyway, he, and countless other molesters, got off lightly if my mother knew about 'their' war. A hateful guest, who pressed his eagerness on my sister in a drunken grope, was excused because he had escaped from Colditz, and so it went on.

On my first day at the chemist shop, a charming old man of about 60 came in, and asked for KY jelly.

'What's it for?' I asked politely.

'Lubrication,' he answered, and I said: 'Of course', as sensibly as I could. When he came to pay, he said he had an account.

'Mister…?' I left a questioning gap.

'Lord actually,' he replied, and I added, 'Lord…?' and left the same questioning gap but with a touch more camp. We laughed, but I was told not to be cheeky with the customers.

'Not even if they're cheeky with me?' I asked, and got halitosis up my nose in a way-too-close advice session as to customer relations, and how I was to be respectful, come what may.

Several sales of talc and Nivea later, a cool sensation rushed in and asked me for *Trojan Life* or similar.

'What's it for?' I asked again.

This time, Major Sleaze the manager said: 'You'll find them in the sports drawer.'

I was flustered, pulled the drawer out too fast and the contents spilled all over the floor. In cartoonish simultaneity, my zip bust and my back burst out. The swell guy took a couple of packets, dropped a five pound note on to the spillage, and fled the scene.

I called after him: 'Your change!' but he was gone, off in a fast car.

The manager caressed my back with tender strokes and suggested I wear an overall.

The next customer was a friend of my mother's, who bought cold cream and remarked on my smart uniform.

The afternoon was no better when David Bowie came in and I hid. I refused to serve him because I was not at ease with my hero. This caused the manager to give me another lecture, on serving the rich and famous with courtesy and discretion.

I imagined serving the rich and famous indiscreetly and laughed out loud. This was insubordination and punishable by suffering more smelly instruction.

The day ended with an accusation. There was money missing from the till. As I knew I wasn't the thief, I answered back that I thought the till should be up, if anything, given the fiver for a couple of packs of johnnies. A stiff silence followed, in which it was explained to me that 'The unfortunate incident in which a customer had not received his change' had already been factored in. It turned out that I'd rung up Lord Wotsit's KY jelly, but he had then put the price of his lubrication on account.

I would be allowed to return if I agreed to take the job seriously, and work on some of my shortcomings.

Today we talk about handsome men. I was recently listening to *Chelsea Hotel* and realised Leonard Cohen sings: '*you preferred handsome men but for me you would make an exception.*' I can't believe anyone would not have found Leonard Cohen handsome, which is probably why I always heard that line as: *You preferred cancer men but for me you would make an exception.*

I love that song. I remember it well, or not so well.

My mother certainly prefers handsome men. 'Come in if you're good looking, stay out if you're not,' was always one of her responses to a knock on the door.

I remark on Samuel Beckett's beauty, and she says she thinks MH★ is a good-looking man, and of course Éamon de Valera.

'But what about Beckett?' I ask. 'What about him?' she answers.

She told the boy who appeared before her in a Paul Jones★ that she was a gypsy and lived in the woods. She was a dark and mysterious schoolgirl who lived on a farm, but her first dance with a handsome medical student sent her into a spin of romance and deception.

I found out about Bantry Roe when I asked her about Beckett. I meant, of course, Samuel Beckett, but she answered with a story about waiting for Beckett the anaesthetist. The story involved a burst appendix and a rush to hospital, where she was shaved *down below* and painted with iodine, with only a little towel covering her breasts.

She was, as she told me, lying there *waiting for Beckett,* who was late, when who should come in but none other than Bantry Roe himself.

'I was so embarrassed. I was mortified and would happily have been swallowed by the table then and there.'

Bantry intensified her shame by greeting her with delight and telling her not to worry, that he would be assisting.

This afternoon she tells the story again, but calls Bantry Roe 'Bantry Bay'. I ask if he was good-looking.

'Very,' she replies.

'How about Mr Beckett the anaesthetist?' 'Not much,' she says.

She says again that MH is a good-looking man, even with his flowing locks, and she laughs. 'And of course Éamon de Valera.'

This reminds her that she has a problem with age, as she is really too old to marry Éamon de Valera.

This is a recurring concern.

Still he is asking her to marry him but she cannot accept because as always she is old enough to be his mother.

I know they had met at a reception in London in the fifties, and that the meeting made a great impression on my mother. She had remarked on his name, asking if he had Spanish blood. He apparently had said he did, and so my mother made her joke about him being a 'Spanish onion in an Irish stew'.

The hostess of the evening had not been pleased with my mother. This is always mentioned, along with the fact that the irate woman was wearing green.

'Green for Ireland, you know, and green for the other…'

The one bit of the story, that I love every time, is: 'He threw back his head and he roared out laughing.'

She tells the story again and I ask if I can record her. I do, and she tells me today, for the first time, that the age difference between them is 35 years.

18

The come and go of these chronicles is on my mind. Boo! The future's behind you.

What about *now*? 'Wake up Marsha.'

DW★ asked me if *Pushing 60* was helping. I laughed. We are no strangers to the outer reaches of reason, us two.

I say I think of it as an experimental work, part of my practice. My *oeuvre*, not therapy. We laugh.

She has just left work for the day, a job in retail. I ask her if her voice has got louder. Rich coming from me, but she ponders and says she thinks it might have done. She notices it gets louder when she's on tour. She's just back, so that must be it.

I ask her about touring in the States, and she says it was 'a wonderful holiday', and how much she loves dancing and singing on a stage for a couple of hours a night. I remark on the obvious, that what she loves *is* her work.

We laugh.

I always told my daughters: 'Don't be with anyone if you don't like who you are when you are with them.'

That was something that came to me in that bicameral★ way, the *other-than* or *sub*conscious way.

I love that interview where Janis Joplin talks about hitching round Brazil like a regular old beatnik. I love that she tells of men and the dangling carrot of their promise, and laughs that beautiful defiant laugh as she tells of going back to her tenth high school reunion. The last laugh is always a lonely-sounding one. I haven't had it, the last laugh, and I don't particularly want it.

I realise I just want to carry on happy. Happy talking with the ones that I love, the lights in the tunnel. Not so long ago, I realised I could not hold out for the big one at the end, but was going to just love the ones already there, lighting up the dark.

I am my mother's daughter. I never knew, truly never knew how much so, till this long encounter with the end of our days.

I too want to tell, and hear, happy stories, to light up the bleak. We know.

'Life can be long,' I say to Silke Thoss★ on our recent trip to Venice, and she thanks me for my alternative view. She is being given all that rush stuff. The snatch-and-grab of it all.

'You can only miss the boat if you believe in the boat,' say I.

What boat and look who's on it? We get on and off real boats with more tourist passengers than locals. How real is this sinking place?

We have a waterproof guide to the city and matching black felt fedora hats. We are not local.

'I am a stranger here myself,' is a fine line for being here at all. In and out of here, who's in and who's out.

In and out of what? Consciousness. Your mind, the crowd.

DW and I met when she was on a float in Oxford Street. I was teaching English as a foreign language and taking beginners on a *point-at-it walk* round Soho. Berwick Street was great for fruit and veg lessons. Look, banana; look, apple; look, potato. A very devout dear boy hid his head in my bosom as we passed the then-frequent doorways to promised sin. It was, I believed, an innocent move on the young man's part.

One of our party was a star-struck girl from Tokyo, who had come to London to meet 'lock stars'. I loved this funny girl and taught her to roll her *aars* round 'rock stars'. Of course, I understood the urgent dreaming that had woken her up and propelled her to London.

We were returning to the Oxford House School of English when she screamed and pointed at a float, decked out with a nautical scene.

The girls in the boat were babes in berets, the docs-and-frocks kind of post-punk girls. One of them was DW and she remembered the TEFL★ teacher *pointing* at them

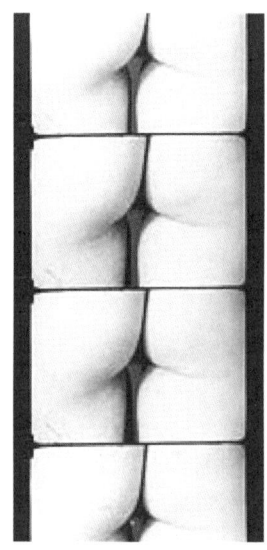

13. *Portrait of Alan*; 14.Yoko Ono, *Bottoms Film no. 4*; 16. *Dressing up*, 1973; 18. *Dolly Mixture and Captain Sensible*, 1982; 17. *Spanish Onion*; 15. *The closest we've been to Vaudeville.*

when later we met, introduced by friends. She said it was most embarrassing, in fact.

Many years later, my husband met Mrs Johnnie Fingers in Tokyo.

It took him a long time to understand what she was telling him, that she was one of my former students. Not just one, *the* one who first pointed me in the direction of my very dear DW.

19

I said something like: 'One day I care, the next I don't. I'm perfect for these days.' I think it was better than that, but I can't remember.

The day before yesterday I was playing a recording of Mick Jones★ talking about his wonderful archive. He is one of the many voices I have collected for *Vox Box*, the seventies jukebox which I am filling with recollections by friends, family, and colleagues, remembering back to being artists, art students or others engaged in cultural production as political action, as social consciousness, reinvention-as-resistance, subordination-as-strategy… back in the seventies.

I had been asked to look at the Acme Gallery archive in relation to the politics of performance, and part of my response was to create a jukebox of all those I know who have good stories, many of which I have heard before.

Art history is full of groups of people who have formed provisional or long-lasting communities. I am not suggesting *Vox Box* represents such a community, but all the voices and stories belong to people I have come across and liked. It's partial and personal, like any record collection.

The jukebox is a good machine in which to house memories. The hits and misses of times gone, and voices alive here today, all set to live on in the acoustic aspic of vinyl.

In the jukebox there is a mysterious circular disc of needles; it is the popularity meter.

My voice isn't meant to be heard on the singles. I try and edit it out, but it gets in when I am recording and want the principal voice to repeat something they have just said off the record, and they have forgotten it, the comment.

'Could you start with *such and such?*' I might say. The idea is that the person remembers and pushes off on their own.

With Mick, I said: 'It was brilliant what you **just** said, about the archive. Can you say it again?'

He said: 'I've forgotten what I said.'

My voice prompts: 'You said it was a burden…'

'Oh yes, I said the archive is a burden to me if I can't share it.'

Such a great sentiment, and almost forgotten.

I hear Gustav Metzger's★ voice in my head, telling his carer to leave us, as it is 'very, very private,' to which I say:

'But this is for a jukebox, Gustav.' 'Am I required to sing?' 'Yes,' I say. We laugh.

I do not include this delightful joke, as I think it is off the record, not *for* the record, and yet here I write it, read it aloud, and, on Friday, I told it in public in the foyer of the British Library as part of an hour-long foyer show involving myself and family. 15 minutes each, with vinyl: *Family Album.*

I often get people to tell stories by telling them their own stories incorrectly. It's not an intentional trick. I would own up to it happily if it were, but I own it as accidental.

I ask X to tell Y the story about *blah blah*, and X invariably says they can't remember it, so I begin, and never get very far, as X remembers and rescues their story and tells it themselves.

I smile as I think of a time I asked my dear friend SR to tell the story of how she had to get rid of Nancy Spungen. She was instructed to take Nancy to the airport and see that she boarded a plane.

It was one of my favourite stories, of no interest to SR herself.

I, on the other hand, thought it was a brilliant story and told it often enough myself. I remember telling it to a boy who showed interest, in the old days.

I was once accused of being Scheherazade by an old flame that flickered on, way beyond the end of love. In his last letter to me, he said that although he had very strong feelings of love for me, they were mixed with pure hatred, and those words were in capital letters.

I was studying how to teach English as a foreign language at the time, so I could go and be with him in Spain, forever and ever. He came into the early chapters, written in 2014. The once great passion turned family friend.

I recently tried to get him to tell a wonderful story which involved him being given a handful of drawings by Andy Warhol. He says he can't really remember it, and has long since lost the drawings, which weren't very good as they were in biro and drawn in very poor light.

'It was something to do with him wanting to meet a boy, who was the beautiful brother of your friend Lourdes,' says I.

'Yes, he did want to hang out with him, I remember.'

'But the brother didn't want to…' I prompt.

'No.'

'And then didn't you ask other guys who Andy Warhol said he would like to meet…?'

'Yes, I asked a few. They weren't interested.'

'Didn't you say he was a very famous artist from New York?'

'I might have done,' says he.

At this point there is no point. It's obvious the story has made much more of an impression on me. I go on, beyond the point where there is none.

'I remember you said he was quite shy,' I urge on.

'Yes, he seemed a nice guy.'

'Was he with Gorka de Duo?'★

'Maybe, yes.'

'And how come he did the drawings for you?'

'I don't know? Maybe to thank me for interpreting, trying to get boys over, or spending time with him.'

'I remember you said he found it a relief that the guys didn't care if he was famous, but you thought he may have just been just saying that, being stoical, and that he was actually quite disappointed.'

'Did I? It's possible.'

After a few more prompts, he suggests it's more my story than his, because I clearly like it so much more.

It was just something that happened once in La Movida Madrileña that I missed because I was having a baby in London. He visited shortly after both events and met us outside the Serpentine. That's when he told me the story, as he thought I might like it.

I loved it.

It was a pleasant gathering. Jem was happy to see he was very small and ugly. From all my talk he was expecting Che Guevara. I think he was what the French might call *jolie laide*. Pretty ugly. He certainly had his charms, and was anyway quite happy to be considered ugly. He would tell anyone that his mother had cried when she first saw him. That is, when he was born.

Later that week he brought his girlfriend to tea. She was wearing a leather string vest.

DW, who I mentioned meeting when she was on a float in Oxford Street, was helping pour tea. We couldn't help but notice one of the girlfriend's nipples, protruding through a hole in her vest. As we refreshed the teapot, we decided it was no accident. Titters, of course. Funny outfit to wear to a lactating woman's place, but it certainly made a point, even if I still don't quite get it.

One night, I asked SR if she would visit the young man to whom I so enjoyed telling stories. I wanted to bring the past to life and introduce him to a living legend. She agreed, but it was very soon apparent that she had no inclination to remember the time when she looked after Sid, when he had overdosed and she lost track of time gazing at tropical fish. I almost told that story word for word, and she said: 'Yes, that sounds about right.'

At last I thought she might remember the Nancy plane story, but she didn't want to go there. This evening must have been in 1998 or '99, and she said: 'I can't remember any of this and, unless I were to look in my diary, which I do not want to do, then it's best forgotten.'

I tried again for *Vox Box*, and I have got a version of the story for the jukebox in which SR remembers Nancy making a phone call to Sid, followed by Nancy's escape. Although she laughs that she can't remember anything, it's a pretty good crack at a story that is now 40 years old.

That night, back in '98 or '99, she did not oblige. She just wanted an evening in the present, a here-and-now encounter with an interesting young artist. I was flustered by my utter failure to prompt any stories and said, apropos of nothing much: 'Whatever happened to Nancy Spungen?'

XX There are two singing bowls in the kitchen and they are inscribed with marvellous names, David Attenborough and Chris Watson, for tonight these two extraordinary persons will be talking to each other at the British Library. The occasion is a *Longplayer Conversation,* which offers an opportunity to consider deep time, and that ever-present unknown to anyone living — the future.

I brought an old tin bottle of Brasso from my mother's flat last year, when I was clearing out all the unwanted stuff. The classic can was full of her daily ritual of maintaining bright brass, from the time when she was still the lady of the house she never owned.

The knocker she rubbed and polished with such vigour is now chromed over in dead good taste, the steps she scrubbed are tiled in black and white.

I think of her laughing at my panic at the time of IRA bombs in Chelsea, and saying I wouldn't have been much good in the war. She told me a story of scrubbing the front door steps and her bucket bouncing over the road as a nearby explosion interrupted her work.

She retrieved her bucket and continued, of course.

I love my mother's wartime stories, which include rescuing a lost white cat, and hiding under a table at The Ritz, or of walking back through the bomb-damaged night and seeing that tins of desirable food had spilled from the broken windows of Sainsbury's on the Kings Road, and how nobody touched them, despite the temptation.

My mother's war is populated with good people, all pulling together. She worked in a florist shop in Mayfair and was clearly a hit with the customers. She tells of a distinguished American coming in to ask for a dozen roses for an officer's wife who had just given birth.

My mother said he asked if he could watch her prepare the roses, so she removed the thorns and cut the stems and arranged the bouquet in front of the American. She told him how she had got them that morning in Covent Garden, and he was most charmed.

I have added the bit about him having been most charmed, as my mother would never say such a thing.

The next day she was told that General Eisenhower sent his compliments and thanks 'to the little Irish girl for a most enjoyable interlude.'

She also told me of another customer who said: 'Call me Bubbles, everyone does,' as he pulled off his cap to reveal a head of white curls. My mother was thrilled to learn that the delightful old gentleman had been the boy in Millais' portrait of blowing bubbles, the painting that became so well known as the Pears soap advertisement.

I loved the stories of a tiny restaurant called the Blue Cockatoo, where fixed price meals were cheaper than making your own dinners. The windows were covered in deep black cloth, but inside the candles lit up the tables, and of course, in my mother's account, everyone was friendly, however important or unimportant they were.

One night, rumour went around that someone very important was coming. It turned out to be Laurence Olivier, so everyone laughed, as he wasn't what they were expecting. I guess they were expecting Winston Churchill.

My mother said Olivier was very good-natured when his arrival was greeted with great mirth and hoots of laughter. She explained he was only an actor, as if an explanation was necessary. I understood.

I think of David Attenborough, who is the same age as my mother and agelessly, brightly present. I once heard him speak and was so bowled over that I lingered around after the talk, just to be near him. I must have been more visible than I had hoped, as he looked round and I was shy to have been caught lurking. I think he just looked without a word, and without a discernible response. It all happened so quickly.

I just remember saying something like: 'Hello… you were… you *are* wonderful… so sorry, I don't want to bug you…' at which point I laughed at my accidental pun and fled.

The singing bowls have been polished with my mother's Brasso.

21 TODAY

Oh David Attenborough, almost the length of the femur of a dinosaur.

Last night's conversation has been on my mind all day. The tiny ferocious war between ants and termites, the sound of victorious clattering, the great expanse of secret land in Argentina where the scattered shells of dinosaur eggs lie like so much broken china junk. The otherworldly sounds of howler monkeys: 'Like a train in a tunnel,' says David Attenborough.

Chris Watson told of being at the North Pole where there is no time. It sounds lonely in all that white space. He stood on top of the world and he thought of his wife.

I was moved, and loved their voices.

Not given to any sense of the supernatural in general, a recording from Attenborough's first visit to Scott's hut in the Antarctic years earlier revealed the uncanny sense of atmosphere he experienced there, and his need to get away from it and go for a walk.

On returning, the hut is full of people and voices. The ghosts have gone.

The recording is hard to hear. It is clearly frustrating for Chris Watson, who is known for exquisite sound.

Kitty★ put the experience of listening to this distressed recording in the living presence of the storyteller into words that I forget exactly, but the gist of her observation nailed the poignancy for me. She said that the story of Scott's haunted hut could easily have been told again by David Attenborough *there and then,* in the present of last night.

'His memory is crystal clear,' she said, 'but seeing him quietly listening to the bad sound recording was profoundly moving.'

Before too long his living voice won't be an option.

I get so excited that later I call the great explorer 'Walter Scott', when I absolutely know he was Robert Falcon Scott. He had lived two doors down from the house of many mentions in Oakley Street.

Later I call termites 'terminites', but maybe I am thinking of us humans.

At my mother's home I tell of hearing David Attenborough speak. He has touched so many lives. Two carers and I talk about the great wonder and relief from the human world that his programmes offer us. One says he started so young, he must have had a career of nearly seventy years by now.

He has given so much and is such a gentleman, the reassuring patrician of erudition, humour and kindness.

I think of this use of privilege and I despise even more the venal worms on top who are giving privilege a bad name and who lack any finer features. This dreadful Bullingdon Club type is beyond all my powers of peace, love and understanding.

The original name of our beloved dog Bonzo was BoJo.

'I'm sorry, I simply cannot call that name across the park,' I said, around this time last year when I visited the puppies. I must have said that with rather too much force for the occasion.

'Oh sorry, are you his godmother?' I asked, sensing an awkwardness. 'His mother is a very good artist,' came the reply.

When I told SR later that day, in an instalment of *My Big Foot and Me*, the never-ending tale, I had just got to the 'Oh sorry, are you his godmother?' bit when she interrupted, without much in the way of intonation, to mention that her sister was in fact his godmother, and that she wished that she had strangled him at birth.

I shrieked out laughing. 'How come your sister is his godmother?!' At Oxford with his mother apparently. Strange breeding ground.

22

My mind is full of men and women and how we become whoever we are.

I am often told wonderful things about a man who menaced me in a long-gone club corridor, cornering me crudely and insulting me with deepest scorn when I made it clear I wasn't playing ball.

I didn't want to be rude or incite more violence.

You don't live with a schizophrenic in your formative years and come through unable to read signs of derangement. The would-be lover said my face was dead. Great chat-up line.

Ever heard of playing possum, creep?

I knew how to play dead or flatter my way out of danger.

To the man who kidnapped me in Italy, I said, stroking his face: 'You could have any woman…'

Behind a locked door for 17 hours, I soothed and charmed, even suggested watching *The Flintstones*, when I saw the cheery stone-agers had come on the set that never stopped.

Clearly an incestuous family, the sister arrived at 4am calling 'Paulo' gently on the other side of the frosted glass.

'*Non stasera*,' he answered.

'I'd like to meet your sister,' said I. But he never opened the door.

I knew not to show my fear. Knew, and know, that he was one of those gentle killers, but I pretended he was a shy passionate type who felt that locking me up was the only way to get me into his home.

And so I reassured him.

I remember saying I would be happy to become the lover of such a beautiful man, but not this way. I would like the door to be open. He said he wanted to watch me sleep, so I pretended, and felt his mad eyes on me as I convinced him by my easy breathing. As if.

His father went off to shoot birds at dawn. I muddled angels (*angeli*) with birds (*uccelli*) and spun out the confusion in beginners' Italian.

'Imagine thinking your father was off to shoot angels…'

One day I might get round to telling the whole story to myself, let alone to another.

I often look up the famous name of my corridor assailant with the words 'sexual assault' beside it, but nothing comes up. He has champions. So many bullies do.

Remembering to be uplifting, I'll play a happy reel.

The great conversation from the night before last is still playing on in my head. I give over to wonder and the natural world and then almost immediately think of the terror among other-than-human creatures, and how I had to say 'This is boring' to a programme about dolphins to which my daughter Ella★ then aged 8 was glued.

She had a picture of a dolphin called Sundance by her bed where I once had Jesus. Thousands of children probably had Sundance watching over them, with his rather smug smile. You could buy him and then he was your dolphin. It was disappointing for her to find he was owned by others. I remember that.

The dolphin show was late, after the watershed. I might have known, but I didn't. We got to the bit about gangbanging and how the male dolphins surround a lone female dolphin and…

Boring was not the word. I couldn't find one.

We ended up watching the nasty Flippers taking turns to be louts. How awful to go so quickly from charm to rape.

Back to David Attenborough.

I once heard him asked which creature was the most engaging, and he answered: 'The three year-old human'.

I have been enjoying such humanity today, as Max, my grandson has been with me. A drawing of him and me says it all: He is big and round and bouncy. I am much smaller than he, and triangular, which is a look I like.

There is a heart in the picture, which is to show that he loves me, he explains.

I think of my mother, always saying how much more sensitive little boys are than little girls, and how I groaned. But I see something of this in a face that moves between expressions of utter joy to extreme despondency in instantaneous flashes.

I laugh at the face of despair as I see a petulant rock star in the tiny boy face, but do everything I can to make it *all better.*

Earlier I had told him not to put cutlery on the table, as the dog jumps on it to bark at the outside world. I talk of dirty paws, and all the places dogs dig, and make points about poo, which is always a winning subject.

Poo bum and away we go…

Smiling face and I pour water from the gurgling fish jug and all is well. The look of lunch had caused sad face. But talk of dirty table tops and dogs' doo chased away the blues.

Must remember: skins on chips are a major downer.

I ask him to say: 'Thank you', not for the unwanted food but for some sugar tongs he likes. I have given them to him 'for keeps' and he is snapping everything happily.

He says he doesn't want them. I understand he'd rather not have them than say: 'Thank you.' He looks like a Gallagher brother, and I suggest an alternative:

He can bow and say: 'Please accept my deepest gratitude.'

I earn a faint smile for my low bow, and a rather cool 'It's ok Marcia, I don't really want them.' No one does.

It's bugging me that the categories of men and women are being used so simplistically. I have never thought anatomy had much to do with it. It's a red herring. I take into consideration kindness, humour, intelligence, compassion, sexiness… it certainly does not have anything to do with genitals or what people choose to do, or not do, with them.

My grandson tells me that his dad says: 'When you are big, you get fur around your willy, but not when you are small.'

I ask if it is fur and he says: 'Maybe hair, special hair'.

Oh yes, the short and curlies by which we are all had in the desperate banality of generalisations.

I am infuriated by generalisations, although often accused of making them. I dream of giving voice to subtlety. Not much time at the moment, but I live in hope.

I remember Katy★ coming round in the pubescent years of the daughters, arriving as we were watching *Sex and the City*. She said it was the most depressing show she'd ever seen, and it was about time we were represented as human beings and not crass versions of gendered idiots manoeuvring for equally irritatingly-drawn men. She ruined that show for us, and rightly so.

It's not a New York I ever knew, nor wanted to know.

It's episode 22 now, and although I've dropped writing by numbers, the grim story from Italy was from when I was 22.

Quack quack, two little ducks, all the twos! I am writing this to the sounds of *Paw Patrol*. 'You get an A for effort, Marsha,' I hear.

Yes, and at least I got out of that room in Perugia, and that corridor. I feel lucky to be sitting next to a dear little human.

23

Dream of a bright little woman talking of terrible hardship in wartime and brandishing a secret weapon. It is lipstick.

Disloyalty plays on my mind because writing about living with a schizophrenic, self-aggrandising aside, lacks subtlety.

As I never tired of telling the German analyst, the trouble with the troubled is that they are often the most sensitive and brilliant. My brother, and many others labelled insane, gave me a way out of a straightjacket that never fitted me well.

I do not romance madness, but am indebted to many who have been on the edge of reason (and beyond) for insights into this life, and a welcome, of sorts, to a way of living it at all.

I remember my brother saying: 'Only civilised people can hurt me,' and I understand the sentiment.

My mother didn't understand madness, but brilliantly referred to herself as '*Exhibit A: The Mother*,' after the head psychiatrist had told her that her son was on the scrapheap of life. This was the morning after her first-born and only son had been taken to a Victorian asylum, under police escort.

A young Irish psychiatrist approached her after she had sat alone on the other side of a table of alienists, as they were once called, and apologised for the way she had been treated.

She had been shocked but, like many innocents facing experts, assumed the cruel prognosis was to be swallowed as the whole truth.

That good young doctor gave my mother the courage to go on that day, and go on she did. She came to meet me so we could go and buy a hamster.

A trades' unionist friend of my father's had turned up a few days earlier and given me ten bob, as he had only just heard of John's death. His name was Stanley, so I told him I was saving up for a hamster and would now be able to buy one outright, and that I would call him Stanley.

My mother always called the hamster Comrade Stanley.

We were on the bus to a Battersea pet shop when she explained that my brother was very ill, using so many roundabout euphemisms that I asked if he was mad.

In a very brave way, she said something approximating an affirmative, to which I said: 'That's good.' She looked at me curiously and asked me why I thought it was good.

'If he had tried to kill you and he wasn't mad, that would not have been good.'

She smiled at me, so I was happy, and I asked her if she thought it would be OK to call a girl hamster Stanley.

By the next year I was not so much into hamsters and never got a second one. I think girls who start young get other ideas halfway through the second hamster, or thereabouts.

This happened to Kitty, who was so devastated by the death of Rockyham that I missed going on an anti-war demonstration.

I neglected political action that day by staying at home to comfort a little girl grieving for a rodent. A Stalinist educator I knew was not amused when I told him this story.

I remember it well. A cross was made out of sticks and a solemn burial took place, followed by recollections of Rockyham, prayers for his onward journey, and songs. Kitty, and Lilly from next door, who was a perfect chief mourner, cried as we celebrated his extraordinary life.

It had been an eventful one, because he had once escaped and lived behind the walls for days. After nearly a week, and no sounds of scratching, he was presumed dead, but turned up unexpectedly one morning in the bathroom and was given a hero's welcome. The second hamster coincided with new interests.

I often recall the point at which Stanley was losing his appeal, and how my friend, who was on to her second, was dimming the lights in her playroom for us to practice close dancing, love bites, and French kissing. She said she chose me to practice with because I was the second best looking. She herself was undoubtedly the most beautiful, and knew it.

Not very much later she went out with David Bowie and pronounced him boring, 'Like those boys who want to be him.' I think he might have liked that. I was in awe of her superiority but said I'd rather not practice, as I thought it might spoil the surprise.

Besides, I was on a mission to understand madness.

I found Freud first, and loved the stories, which I devoured like who-dunnits.

R.D. Laing, who I found on my brother's bookshelf at the time of the Troubles, came after Freud and made a big impression.

Although much later I erupted in a fury when I railed against the celebrity status of *the one* and thought – and still think – everyone in a dysfunctional family deserves compassion, if not actual help.

Still, Laing was a great charismatic force and I loved his stories. He once told of seeing a billboard in California: *Keep your passage honeymoon fresh, have a Caesar.*

He articulated the madness of the world and of the so-called sane brilliantly. I attended some meetings of the Philadelphia Association as I wanted to be in the presence of a living grown-up who objected to ECT. I was demented by the thought of this treatment, and my brother's poor head being shocked against his will.

He wrote on the cover of a Lion's brand notebook: 'JDS Farquhar, b. 1946, d. 1971'. ★

My brother once told a visitor to Banstead, the Victorian asylum, that he was worried our mother was raising me to be the bride of Prince Charles. I laugh at this sometimes, and it crossed my mind today when a carer in my mother's home asked me if I was excited about the wedding. She meant the Royal Wedding.

I said I wasn't particularly interested, but added: 'My mother loves that sort of thing,' so as not to sound like a snob. Luckily she said she wasn't interested either, but thought Harry was doing it for his mother.

I checked the carer meant Diana and was rather moved by this interpretation, the idea of living on happily ever after for the ones who can no longer.

My mother was happy today and told me some wonderful stories. She told a great one about a truck of Fyffes' bananas crashing into a derelict gate lodge, and how all the bananas flew up into the trees and across the fields, and how the driver invited everyone to help themselves.

Following this, she remembered my father taking an enormous bunch of bananas to someone called Brooke, and how Brooke was overjoyed by receiving such a gift.

I remarked that Brooke was an unusual name, and I had only ever met one.

'Brooke Evans,' she said, and then mentioned Scott of the Antarctic because Brooke Evans' father had been one of Scott's team. She said that Scott had lived in Oakley Street, two doors down, and I said I had been thinking of that recently, and asked who lived there when we were there.

She said: 'All sorts,' but that when she had first arrived it was a brothel and the woman who ran it was 'rather charming'.

I asked her if she remembered the Polish prostitute from next door, who gave me the most wonderful clothes I've ever owned, and my mother said: 'Oh, she was a beautiful girl, and much loved. Sybil Thorndike adored her.'

We got on to Sybil Thorndike,* who used to ask my mother to lunch, just to hear her voice. My mother said that she used to say: 'I cannot get over your beautiful voice, remarkable coming from the bog as you do.'

My mother was laughing at this. 'I wasn't quite from the bog, but she seemed to love thinking that of me.'

I remember Dame Sybil's enormous enthusiasm for my mother. She obviously had a love of characters and was actually very kind about my brother's illness. I always remember the kindness of people at that time. It's for this reason I know that privilege can be used well, and why I still love such people who do good.

My mother fed Bonzo biscuits and said he had 'brought me untold happiness.' I quote.

I told her that I had tried, and failed, to photograph the first snowflake I had ever seen on him.

'There'll be more snow,' she said, and laughed.

24

I've been smelling warm milk for days in the place where I write.

At first I thought someone nearby was cooking milk for a coffee and found it comforting.

Over the last few days the scent of milk has deepened queasily. I have presumed it to be the ghost of a smell, because no milk enters this space. When perplexed, I file under *mystery*, and proceed.

I remember once hearing that the Chinese say Westerners stink of rancid milk. Maybe it's just the stink of the West.

Oh, how I hated the warm milk of childhood. Those little bottles, that *Thatcher, Thatcher, milk snatcher,* stole from all her children, as they are known. The generation, after my own, who grew up with this absence, only to suck it up in lattes, flat whites and cappuccinos.

I think of Thatcher with such anger, but I have never met one child of the sixties who enjoyed the morning milk. I always volunteered myself as milk monitor so by the time I'd handed them around, time was up, and I could avoid the most unhappy drink I have ever known.

The mystery stench turns out to be cheese I took from the dinner after the talk at the British Library.

A woman on the tube asked me if my dog was a *cockapoo* and I said, avoiding the term *schnoodle*: 'He's three quarters poodle and a quarter Schnauzer.'

She looked like Una Stubbs, a petite, bright woman, about ten years older than myself. She asked his name and I said he was Bonzo, 'originally BoJo', and told how I couldn't have called out *that* name across the park.

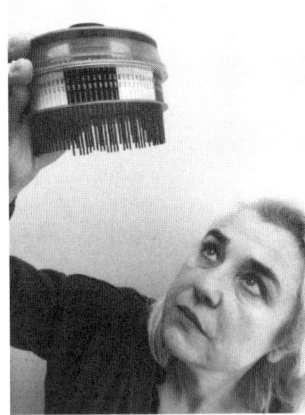

19. *Popularity Meter*; 20. *Brasso*; 22. *Marshall*; 24. *Through a milk bottle*; 23. *First Hamster*; 21. *Dog and bowl.*

Her face closed, she got up, and without a word, stood facing the doors midway between stations. I called after her, 'Lovely to have met you!' but answer came there none.

We are in tricky times. Not just apocalyptic ones, but in everyday peril. Oddness is accelerating and there are too many reasons to keep out of trouble and conversation.

A much-loved person in my life tells me how the real Boris Johnson is the brightest, warmest, and most humorous person, and how I would love him if I met him. I fear that might be so. I have met charming despots.

Or one, anyway, the Argentinian husband of one of my students back in the TEFL days, a year or so before the Falklands War, as it was called in England.

I had invited my class to go to a jumble sale as they always asked about my clothes. My Argentinian student's husband wanted to come, and so he did, and my Spanish then-boyfriend, an exile from Franco's Spain, refused to talk to him.

'You are so naïve. He is high up in the regime,' he said to me. 'Is he?' I said. 'Well, he's very nice.' 'Of course he is.'

Actually, the husband understood the silence very well, told me not to worry and left. His wife apologised for her very existence and I bought her a cup of tea from the good old-timers of long-gone Chelsea jumble sales.

When the war broke out, an Eritrean boy, who everyone loved, sang *Don't Cry For Me Argentina* and we all laughed, except the lovely Argentinian woman, who wept.

We all went for tea, and there was much comfort exchanged in broken English.

Anyway, I just wish the real Boris Johnson would step out from behind the dangerous bluster and be compassionate, at least.

My brother writes that he is frightened and bewildered. 'Me too,' I reply.

Me too is such a funny, babyish couple of words.

Yesterday I met up with an old friend,★ a marvellous painter who was a great flame of the seventies, much revered and desired. Her stories are so extraordinary, and delivered in such a deadpan way, that I could listen all day and all night. She wants to get back to paint, and leaves me wanting more.

Earlier in the day, in a phone call, she says it is hard to talk as she is painting. I call her a 'real artist' and it's not a joke.

We discuss solitude and how valuable it is. I know this is the key to the future, as a personal matter, keep time, keep your time.

She mentions a legendary, now-dead artist, and wonders about telling of a very bad experience in the spirit of *Me too*.

The dead are gone, and, besides, not many would ever have accused her unbidden lover of being a gentleman, or a gentle man. They all have their champions of course. Fame and the sycophants.

And the other camp: Fame and the begrudgers.

Funny it's become such a raging ambition. My sister-in-law, who is a head-teacher, not headmistress ('So public school, Marcia'), says it often comes up in answer to the question: 'What do you want to be when you grow up?'

'Famous'.

'Famous for what?'

She prompts with the obvious: for science, for dancing, for painting, for healing, for helping … but draws a blank.

This is a blank, a great void, and one which I fear is extremely convenient to apolitical and right-wing forces. Where are the train drivers, teachers, nurses, doctors, builders, painters, space travellers, singers and fire-fighters in the dreams of childhood?

I admire my friends who have fame as a by-product of doing what they had to do, and doing it seriously and well. It takes dedication, and it takes its toll. I think of paying a price for being paid a price and wonder.

I'm feeling old today, and done in. I am writing on, beside my sleeping mother. I hear a voice saying to the ever-groaning lady: 'Why all the crying darling?'

There is never an answer, but the enquiry is so kind and the voice so soothing. The home is a place to witness real kindness, and know it's real because it's given to all the residents by carers who earn so little money and, even more wrongly, so little respect for their labour.

I mean so little respect from the bullies in power, those who give privilege a bad name.

My mother cries out in my direction: 'Go away and take the light with you.'

I close the curtains and ask her to open her eyes, and she sees Bonzo★ and says: 'Ah, you dear boy,' and to me: 'You'd be lost without him.'

I laugh, as I am feeling lost today, and she says: 'No joke.' I answer: 'No joke.'

25

Despot was not the word.

I kick myself that I used the wrong word, as I am not as devil-may-care as I might appear to be about words. I have been punished enough for writing too fast and like a fool. I see the origins, the wonder and the shame of it.

My mother once stayed on when everyone had left a Sunday drinks party, saying we had been asked to lunch.

I said I didn't think we had. We muttered it out. I asked her under my breath for the exact wording of the invitation. It turned out we had been invited to 'drinks *al fresco*'. My mother had taken this to mean lunch.

'Lunch *al fresco*,' she said, by way of explanation. 'That means lunch outside,' I explained.

'Oh, crikey,' said my mother, and we hurried off.

I once corrected, with some urgency, 'Capability' under my breath, as my mother had just called the legendary garden designer *Calamity* Brown.

I was often embarrassed given that I moved about in the top drawers. Luckily, the ones that I inhabited were often enlightened and mostly populated by those kind to the less fortunate.

Katy understands this deeply, and decodes a photograph where I, aged 6, look balefully out from her sister's grand birthday tea and know I will never get Mr Miles and his vanishing rabbit for my birthday, or a screening of *The Red Balloon*.

I laugh when I remember, for the first time in over fifty years, what I did get: my mother and sister, behind the sofa, pushing up the puppets from a fifties toy box. This was in the sixties, off the King's Road.

There was a glass coach drawn by a real pony at Sarah Worsley's party. All the children took turns to ride round the drawing room, waving and smiling.

The unbearable delight of others was hardly endurable. Only the promise of being *the real Cinderella,* for a turn around the almost-Royal room, kept me breathing.

And then, shockingly suddenly, it was home-time for the tired pony.

I was brave about the turn that never came, because I thought my mother would have been sorry for me, and that, of all her many responses, was the most unbearable.

I learned to loathe the snobs, who crushed her willingness to join in, and loved the welcoming ones of all persuasions.

I once told her that she had been best-befriended by homosexuals and libertines.

'I have to say, you make a good point,' said my mother who had dubbed herself 'the virgin widow' at 41. No wonder she was a hit with the homos, as she called her male friends, even when the word gay had come into everyday usage.

Her old friend Richard Goolden★ wrote to the *Times* at the time of this new coming, objecting to young homosexuals calling themselves 'gay' when they looked so miserable.

I never actually saw the letter, but he was of a generation to romance the illicit, and he was old-school.

I loved 'Call me Mole or Moley, but never Richard, do you understand?' and I still treasure a drawing he did of himself as Mole in *Toad of Toad Hall,* a role he played for 50 years. Come to think of it, that drawing is in biro.

I went, year after year, to the dress rehearsals of *Toad,* and can still see him skipping on to the stage with his hands moving together in a rhythmic gesture of Moleish excitement.

'Oh my, oh my, oh my!'

Once, he tried to guilt-trip my mother and me, who had tickets to see *Bent* at the Royal Court. We encountered Richard. (I never liked calling him, or any human, by an animal name) outside the theatre. He was unable to get a seat and told us that it was probably more up his street than ours.

'Well you certainly *are* up our street, darling Richard,' said my mother, and to me:

'Take no notice,' which made me laugh.

He lived at the top of Oakley Street so we were on the same bus on the way back and my mother congratulated him on getting in to see the play.

'Well, they know me there, of course.'

'Of course they do darling,' said my mother, as if she was humouring a fantasist.

I think he had played Nagg. Anyway, he was a good friend of Samuel Beckett's, and not just any old man when it came to going to the theatre.

Cecil Brock★ was another of my mother's friends in Oakley Street, who she had known a long time. He'd been at the Abbey with one of her sisters. James Mason had lodged with his mother in Dublin when Cecil was still Patrick. I never met 'James', but heard enough about him.

I have always loved the charismatic friends-to-the-stars. One rarely meets the famous other, which is good, as they might get in the way of the story. The stories are affectionate and always reflect well on the storyteller, the lesser or unknown one.

I relate to this. Jem tells me not to call myself 'a pivotal nobody'. I think it is a good category, which I invented for others, and then included myself.

I do own up to problems with proper names. And improper naming and name-dropping.

No such problems for Cecil. We would listen for hours to tales of Katherine Hepburn and Vivien Leigh, and couldn't have given a hoot as to the veracity. My mother and I loved a good story and never measured the quantity of hot air.

'And what I don't know, I'll make up,' was a little phrase I often heard my mother add to 'I'll tell you all when we meet…'

One of my favourites was a Dublin story.

Patrick, as was, and James, were on a tram when Maureen O'Hara★ got on. James was all ready to greet her, but as Cecil told me: 'I had to stop him; we didn't have money for her fare.'

There were more exciting ones, like when an ancient tortoise he was minding in a mansion in the Hollywood Hills crawled over a ravine edge and smashed to its death. I don't know if that was Hepburn's turtle, or whose, but it did have a star owner who might have inherited it from Cecil B. DeMille or Orson Welles.

When Cecil met my mother and me in the street, he would always say, after greeting his little sister in Christ, 'We must spare the child,' a witty inversion of that old *spare the rod* dictum that implied their grown-up conversation was dull. It never was.

He lived up the King's Road end of Oakley Street, the Richard Goolden end, opposite David Bowie and the once-home of Oscar Wilde's mother.

Cecil's basement flat smelled of cat urine and aftershave, a combination I have always associated with a certain glamour, and have always relished.

Cecil ended his days in the actor's home, which my mother said was a good thing as he 'loved that sort of thing.'

Funny remark to make about someone who had dedicated their life to a profession, but she always had an unusual way with words. She once called the Kennedys 'A sad little bunch' when Cecil and I were listing their tragedies.

We laughed. I suggested 'tragic dynasty' might be more apt. 'This is the genius of your mother,' he told me.

'Go on,' said my mother, which is a great way of telling someone to stop talking nonsense you're enjoying.

When Cecil was dying, a nurse mistook my mother for his wife. 'No,' said my mother, 'he got away.'

He was very near the end and she got up on the bed, cradling his head, as they had asked her to get him to drink.

She said: 'I had to laugh at being taken for the wife of one of the finest homos I have ever known.'

26

I find myself awake at the hour before dawn and it is dark. It makes me recall my quip: 'This dawn *is* the darkest hour,' when Donald Trump got into power.

At least no one has popped up to tell me how I would love him if I only knew him.

No one in my circles has a good word for the President of the United States, except my mother, who has said he makes her laugh.

Apparently he appeals to dementia sufferers – no joke (though no science either). One carer and one elderly niece of a resident concurred.

It is curious, in an NHS home, to have news pumping out non-stop, frightening accounts of the health service, both here and there, alongside moving images of apocalyptic situations, and then the next princess, coming soon to a blaring set in your home.

'She looks just like the other one,' I say.

'Don't make me laugh,' says William, one of the residents. Even my mother seems to have forgotten the Royals.

Trumped and Tangoed, laughter is probably the best response. I have heard derisory laughter is the scorn that does the trick.

Not that I can imagine despots losing sleep over ancient care home people roaring their heads off.

William repeats his instruction to me: 'Don't make me laugh,' when I say: 'Some say we come back again.'

I said this in answer to a lovely old lady who says '*Delicious*' after each and every crisp. She tells me that we might as well enjoy all things because we only live once.

I ask my mother if she likes Irish music when I see her tapping along, and she says she likes her biscuit.

'Not the pap, not the pap,' she cries out later, 'it makes me sick.'

I'm sure Nagg and Nell are fed pap.

A carer and I say it looks nice. 'Solid and soft,' I say.

Funny combination. I might go for a leader who promised to be solid and soft. My arse.

Just received a picture of a Peckham liberal club interior.

'Ghastly looking place, can't wait,' I reply, and see why some people object to my voice. Probably why theatre people have been so understanding.

A bearded comrade, at a *Not in My Name* concert where I was intoning the war crimes of Tony Blair, asked me if I was an actress.

'No, I am not an actor,' I replied clearly, to which the comrade said: 'At least that is something,' as if I was applying with suspect credentials to be a party faithful.

'I am not a member of The Revolutionary Communist Party of Britain (Marxist/Leninist) either,' said I, and that silenced the beard.

Not so long ago, a chipper-voiced young fundraiser phoned on behalf of the Labour Party and thanked me for my loyal membership, so I said it wasn't so loyal.

'I also support the Green Party, and,' I said, 'I voted Remain.'

'Fantastic,' she said, and I asked: 'What, fantastic as in unbelievable, or as in very very good?' I didn't get an answer.

We moved swiftly on to any comments about the party that could be useful to Jeremy. I asked where the party stood on Brexit and she said: 'Jeremy is very keen to hear from you, but I have exceeded my time.'

'How much time did you have?' I asked.

She didn't answer that either, but asked about the possibility of a donation.

To which I replied: 'Fantastic, thank you so much for your time, and all the best to you and Jeremy.'

I look at my mother and I know I learned a lot of this cheek from her, but she restrained herself. She objected to the cruelty of her sister's ability to turn another's misfortune into a joke, and warned against it.

My aunt, Toffee O'Drooler of *The Londoners*,★ played so memorably by Kitty Finer, once gave some poor relations, a pair of dull sisters, the names Flesh and Blood. My mother sprang to their defence; they were good women, dedicated nurses, and very devoted to their mother.

Their real names have long gone, but I can see the funny side of Flesh and Blood as names for unloved relations.

This aunt called me Ivy, on account of my attachment to my mother.

She called me a communist. Yes, it's all relative. Wishy-washy liberal to a grand Stalinist, red hot Commie to a Tory aunt.

I once heard Kitty answer: 'No, it *was* my fault.'

I asked her what had been her fault. She had been answering the question: 'Have you been involved in an accident that wasn't your fault?'

27

We did a lot of laughing in those dark days. Some of it was nervous, but my brother was always good with words.

'Bend my rubber arm,' he once said, as I offered him a drink. He had already had way too many.

I think of Sylvia Plath and all her beautiful luggage, her perfection in appearance, her brilliant brain and, of course, ECT.

I wonder if the other two are still alive, the others who waited at the party while Ted and Sylvia went all the way in the next room.

Blooded and fierce, I see them leave that room. No walk of shame, no fall. Not then.

I have always seen that scene, and felt it somehow. I know what losing a father in childhood can do.

I never had the perfect luggage, nor the harsh genius of Sylvia, which is probably just as well. I drew myself through much pain, odd drawings looking like Cocteau's or Lorca's. Curiously enough, writers' drawings.

Anyway, mothering and suicide. I went off track.

By the age of 27 I was the mother of two, and left out of the life I had dreamed alongside the bright boys. What is it with the bright boys and the tin-pot Svengalis…

I, Theresa…

Great one that. I meant Tiresias of course. I did sort of perceive the scene and foretell the rest. Two unanswered requests to talk on the real radio about my part in the past are on my mind now, right now.

'You can never go back,' says my mother, who goes there all the time. I'm with her, following the onwards sign onwards in all directions.

I tell Jem that I remember when Ella was born as if it was last night. He says he is not surprised. I remember out loud, watching *The Twilight Zone* on a black and white TV, waking him up, putting on an old man's mac. What an outfit. Just a flasher's mac and stilettos.

I have a memory of the antenatal catalogue the hospital gave being by our bed. The couple on it were playing Scrabble. I cried because Jem wouldn't play Scrabble and we couldn't be like them. I wonder where they are now.

Alone when I woke at night, I snip-snip-snipped at fifties National Geographics and Mothercare catalogues, making disturbing hybrid birth images. Collages that perished, in a damp coal hole, in the late eighties.

I remember the hospital, the same where I had been born. The Middlesex in Goodge Street.

My mother often talks about my birth, and me as a baby. I think of her carrying a baby she intended to give away, and how the near-death of my birth might have caused the change of heart.

I think of the past of the dead: the old dead, the new dead and the coming dead. I'm always curious as to who is clutching the parcel when the music stops. Who buries the dead, who tells the living?

I am advised to write something about my mother, in advance of her death. A half-baked eulogy is on my mind. It is uplifting of course, so uplifting that it makes me cry.

Yesterday, my mother told me she had been abandoned and cried to be taken home. I heard it deeply, although she was only talking about being left in the lounge with the silent residents and the blaring TV.

She said: 'It's so boring,' and I remember how she cried this same word in terror, back when she had fallen for the last time. She was demented by the idea of the television, particularly the smiling 'Cruella' with her 'cookery class'.

I asked her why she found it so frightening.

'It's so boring,' she said. I didn't ask her for a synonym.

It was at this time that I said: 'This is like Beckett,' and she replied: 'He knew… poor man.' He did indeed, and I'm beginning to get a pretty good idea myself.

How lovely that bitter means please in German, and gift is poison. I muse on gifts and how it's brave to rub the lamp, open the box, to do whatever it takes to unleash the evils, as they are called in most accounts of the contents of Pandora's box.

After all the evils comes hope, maybe the cruellest of the lot. Hope hurts.

But I wish it on myself, and others, and share the instruction that I received from wherever, one hopeless, desperate day.

'Recalibrate hope,' said the voice, mine, to myself. Some would say the angels spoke, but I'd just say it was one of my own coming through with a bit of advice.

Spending time with our friend Esperanza recently, she said: 'You didn't know Woody,' and she gave me a beautiful drawing of him and her husband from way, way back.

Maybe I did know him. *What's in a name?* I think, and remember that I called my mother Hope in the soap opera of our lives.

28

And here comes Christmas, barrelling along.

Almost deafened by *Jingle Bells* on the tube, *jingle jangle*. My head is hurting and the sound of this song is giving me bad vibrations. I notice it's being sung by a man of my age. I don't want him to see my pity.

The Amnesty group singing gentle *loo la loo lay* type harmonies at the top of the escalators are raising money for people living in unimaginable horror, and, just below, a man of my age sings of jingle bells, wearing a smile-face.

'It is called a *winter fair*, Marcia,' says Olive.

I love the baby and the star, the shepherds and wise men, the Magi and the idea of an alternative to wealthy birth with all the trimmings.

I'm not religious, but I love animals even more now I am pushing 60, and can think of nothing lovelier than a human birth among creatures. And such a great mixed crowd of humans, too.

I am rather saddened by the thought that Christmas could cause offence. Why now? Nonbelievers, or believers in other creeds, used to wish *happy holidays, season's greetings* or *bah humbug*, but they didn't try to get rid of Christmas.

I think only Oliver Cromwell succeeded in doing away with it, but that was only because he was so sure that it was a carnal carnival, disrespectful to his lord Jesus, who was never a messiah I wanted to know.

'Jesus is great for kids,' a sound man once said. I agree, except the bit about his death. I was broken-hearted every Good Friday, and never believed in the Resurrection. I believed in all and nothing.

'How can a fat man get down a chimney? What if there is no chimney? If he is everywhere at once, how come he was at Arding and Hobbs?* Was that the real one?'

'No,' said my sister.

'Who is the real one?'

'There isn't one.'

'What?!'

I went to ask my parents, and they agreed there wasn't one.

I didn't care so much about Father Christmas, but I did love Jesus, so I asked:

'When do I get to know Jesus isn't real?'

My grandmother was sure this was further evidence of the devil within my heathen heart, while my father hissed his laugh of cold mirth and I found myself in another domestic dilemma, at home in a schism.

Jesus suffered the little children, and was famously friendly to lepers, prostitutes and poor people. What's wrong with that?

Maybe the appeal of Jesus could be given more thought than snooty dismissal, or worse, cynical lip service, by some of our church-going leaders.

I loved those lines of Leonard Cohen's:

'When he knew for certain only drowning men could see him, he said all men will be sailors...'

It seems quite convenient to take away the Christmas message and forget about the eye of the needle and the camel passing through, even more of a challenge than Old Fatty with his sack of crap, coming down a chimney near you.

Winter wonderland and candy cane joy. Bah, humbug.

I don't have any advisors on this runaway train of thought, but Jem lends me an ear sometimes. I just read this one out to him and he said he was glad it was called the winter fair and that I sound like a Brexiteer with my nostalgia for Christmas and the true message.

He says he thought I was a pagan, and I said: 'What, me?'

And after a pause added: 'I do love candles, hooch, and a bit of mayhem, if that's what you mean.'

He seemed to approve of my last sentences, where there is some evidence that I am more *with it*. Here they are:

I fear being a downer, but I can't help it. A time for the kids, eh? Children, I learned, do not belong to those who have given birth. The ownership trip is a disaster.

A cheering old assistant in the pharmacy where I waited for my mother's medication last Christmas, began a rant against the do-gooders who suggest we all take in a refugee.

'What cheek!' she gasped, between sharing pleasantries on the marvel that is Prince Phillip with another customer who was buying adult nappies.

I sank beneath my own opinion with a heavy heart, that piece of the mind that knows no peace. How to answer the kind lady who is happy that Trump is leader of the free world, just himself and his finalists…

I remember saying: 'I think it could be good, like the inn-keeper offering his stable.' She said: 'Your blister packs are ready.'

29

I am awake in the middle of the night, and angry with my mother for being so rude to Christine Keeler in the lift of a block of mansion flats when we were visiting one of our better-off relations.

I thought she was beautiful, a bit like the lady in the sweet shop, who I can still see surrounded by gum-pink and tangerine swirls.

The tall woman in the lift was smiling at me, and remarking on my appearance in some complimentary way, when my mother abruptly turned me 180 degrees so I was faced away from the source of pleasure.

My mother was odd about compliments, and never agreed with people if they said I was pretty, but she didn't usually twist me like a screw-top in the opposite direction.

When I turned to say goodbye, my mother pulled at me again, as if in a hurry to deliver me from evil.

The woman gave me a kind smile, and I wished she had rescued me there and then. I would have loved her to have been my mother.

It was bad enough that my own mother wore Hush Puppies and skirts to the knee, and that her total lack of modernity was a constant embarrassment, but at least she was friendly, and, much to my relief, people seemed to quite like her.

But this uncharacteristic hostility upset me. I asked my mother why she had turned my face away from the pretty woman. It was in this way I learned about what was then called the Profumo affair.★

My mother explained the terrible risk to our national security caused by the woman in the lift. She might as well have been telling me about the woman in the sweet shop. I listened to a really dull account of the embarrassment and pain it had caused his poor wife, the humiliation, *blah blah*.

It really goes to show that the most sensational story can be reduced to the dullest distillation.

It was one of my mother's nastiest days, and I always wanted to apologise on her behalf to Christine Keeler, whose obituary I have just read.

She was shy and knew shame, probably what made her so sexy, along with her long hair, long legs, and gentle face.

Mandy Rice-Davies was soon back up in the top drawers, gobby and iconic. 'He would, wouldn't he?' wasn't her only line. But not the lovely Christine, wounded by sadness and shame.

I can remember her warm shyness, and later what I would be able to call sexiness, from that very brief encounter in a lift in Shelley Court, Tite Street.

Tite Street, where Oscar Wilde had lived, and where I had had my tonsils out the very same year that John Profumo denied impropriety and, like Wilde, did not get away with it.

'Poor devil, he did a lot of good at Toynbee Hall,' my mother said, much later, when the film came out.

We knew all about Toynbee Hall because my brother went to a drama group there when he was recovering from treatments. My mother would warm his coat by the gas fire and we would wave the reluctant actor off to Toynbee, which he always said in a funny voice, as if he was a zombie.

'Toynbee'.

One night, he returned and told us a funny story, which was a wonderful sign of him coming back.

A man in the group had been asked to smoke a cigarette in character. He had said: 'I am not a smoker as a rule, but I will smoke a cigarette for this role.'

After a pause he added, seriously: 'Anything for art'.

My mother, brother and I fell about laughing at this, and used it as a catchphrase ever after, for as long as we were all together.

Christine Keeler's is a sad story, and one that might easily have gone unknown, but for another sexy situation ending in gunshots at the osteopath's house.

Someone mentioned in the obituary as responsible for bringing the scandal to light, appeared in Oakley Street later on in the seventies.

Gunshots and ganja, along with other risks to national security, were not my mother's thing at all, but Aloysius Lucky Gordon would become one of her doorstep friends. Scrubbing steps and polishing the knocker was a great way into conversations with all sorts.

'The Jamaicans', as my mother called them, passed her house on the way to play football in the park, and said hello to her of course.

The Spanish once-boyfriend had been with a Moroccan prostitute before he met me, getting it for free. She lived in Oakley Street and knew the all-male household at no. 42.

This was how come I knew who they were, quite early on. It was soon an open secret, like the whereabouts of Salmon Rushdie, but way more sexy.

Much later, when my mother was in a rehab out west, off Ladbroke Grove, a carer called Ignatius lit up her life and asked her to adopt him.

She said: 'Aloysius, I would be honoured.'

My mother is sleepy today and my lumbago is killing me.

I don't mention Christine Keeler to her, but look up Profumo while she is sleeping, and see he was a member of the Bullingdon Club.

I notice chunks of gilt and plaster have fallen off the frame around my brother.

'He's been off the wall,' I say to a carer I like, and she says: 'Looks like it.' I mention it to my mother, who says: 'He wanted to get out.'

'But came back,' I add.

'Looks like it,' she says, quite calmly, and doesn't mention the imminent death of one whose portrait has fallen off the wall.

Phew.

HALFWAY TO 60

Have been in pain. I am quite sure it's the psychic load that has doubled me up, but Katy says my handbag is too heavy. Jem has said the same, and the osteopath agrees, and asks me if it's full of lipstick.

'It is not,' I answer archly, and turn down his next suggestion with: 'I do *not* want to carry my load in a bum bag.' He cheers me up.

We had supper with a new-70-year-old last night, who says it is a much more enjoyable age than 60. I guess it's all bonus time after 70, if you count the three score years and ten.

'I'm not dreading 60,' I say, 'just finding it a bit of a number.'

As to what has happened to my back, I explain that: 'I leave bits of me in the traps.'

Luckily I only eat with people who understand the difficulty some of us have giving straight answers.

I haven't set out to give tips, but what's the point of having lived so long if you haven't got anything helpful to say. It is a good idea to only eat with those who wish you well and you wish the same.

I get this idea of wishing-well from a friend★ who has well-earned her many accolades, and weathered her brickbats with impressive restraint and the greatest of good humour.

It was after seeing her that I had the dream of the lady with the secret weapon, lipstick. We discuss getting away from the be-grudgers.

'Fuck the be-grudgers,' said Brendan Behan, and there was a man who knew.

I think of my mother being taken to see *Richard Cork's Leg* by an unmarried lodger in his fifties, five years after she was widowed, and how she had been mortified when there was a long passage on widows ('widders') being desperate for it.

I recall my mother speaking quite plainly to me about her embarrassment. She was very keen to protect me from low life, while managing to communicate a lasting memory of a sex-mad blind man in a graveyard, fucking a line of widows.

I never did find that scene in the play, but something early on about a stone erected by a widow, after her one night of marriage, gave me a clue as to what might have caused the trouble. *'Came and went,'* was the inscription on the grave.

I could see how this alone might have meant a most uncomfortable outing to the theatre for a landlady widow.

My mother said she had known nothing of the plot when she had chosen it, and told me the poster outside the Royal Court, had described it as 'an entertainment from Dublin with a bit of music.'

I can't wait to write fiction so that I can honestly say that my characters bear no relation to anyone living or dead. I will write the proclivities of some I have known into stories that will astound, shock, sadden, sicken and entertain.

But not yet. This *Pushing 60* is based on some semblance of the truth as I recall it, from last night and long before that, from other people's accounts and my mother's dictation, diction, commentary running — as it does— continuously through my head.

I never knew Bethlehem was only five miles from Jerusalem. I looked up the topical locations in the middle of a sore night and shivered at Trump's apocalyptic gift to the world. I looked up the word *intifada* and learned it also means shiver.

I was happy to hear from the new 70-year-old that it is a much more enjoyable age than 60, and remembered that I felt the oldest I ever felt at 30. I had to take valium to go to my own party.

A well-known female singer, who I didn't know, asked me whose party it was, and I said it was mine. 'Who are you?' she asked. 'No one you know,' I said.

One thing that pleased me is that my good friends all came back to our flat, with the caged gas fire and the shelves of toppling toys, and that included the famous ones who had been the cause of the influx of scenesters in the first place.

I remember loyalty, and how much I always valued it, and continue to value it.

25. Richard Goolden, *Mole End*, 1966; 26. *Peckham Liberal Club*, 2017; 29. *Toynbee Hall selfie with Franko B*, 2014; 28. *Mabin,* 1968; 30. *Richard's Cork Leg*, Royal Court Theatre, 1972; 27. Marcia Farquhar, *Miximatoto*, 1975.

31

Loyalty has got me worrying. Particularly blind loyalty.

Such use of blind now sounds offensive to the actual blind, but what is a synonym for a lack of 20/20-visioned superiority? *Blinkered* might be a more sensitive word for unquestioning loyalty.

Loyalty to the crown, the church, the toadstool. The family.

An appeal to this type of loyalty is supposed to hush any complainers, to keep secrets and injuries behind the closed doors of all sorts of institutions.

At the end of number 30, I commended those who chose to go to the humble homes of their friends rather than to the flasher haunts of the scenesters. I was praising a certain loyalty in a certain context, and being self-deprecating.

This is *not on* at any age, let alone pushing 60. I have often warned others from demeaning themselves.

I can't go back and read that again so I thought I would add a more upbeat note: It isn't loyalty, it's *love*. And knowing where's best, where you can roar out, pass out, dry out, laugh out, cry out, or be silent.

It's being among friends, and it's that which I have valued so much, and valued those who know it and show it, and ever more so now.

Loyalty was an odd word, and has been on my mind, so much as to wake me up.

I wouldn't want anyone hearing this to think I am on the side of the blinkered loyalty that causes people to defend the dangerous deeds of their friends and relations in the name of family or religion.

I have had my own problems with loyalty, every which way.

Punished with exclusion for my inappropriate laughter in prayers at Brownies at an early age, I have always feared such oaths of allegiance.

I didn't know if I was meant to be pledging my troth to the Queen or the toadstool, an easy mistake. And so I laughed out loud and was offered *'one more chance'*, the ultimate side-splitting line to anyone in the throes of illicit convulsions.

SR said she could see me as a flag-waving berk when I told her my mother used to take me to see the Trooping of the Colour. My mother never gave me a flag of course.

It wasn't usual for children from my school to be taken on such outings. If they went to anything royal it was more usually as friends of the family.

My mother and I were an unlikely pair. Other children called me posh when they heard me speak, and asked me why I wasn't up on the balcony. I was very hurt by this, but my mother said: 'Take no notice, they mean no harm, and besides, you do have a very clear voice.'

I think of my mother and Bernard Cheeseman, a friendship that began way back in the fifties when my brother and sister were removed from the Lycée in South Kensington to go to an LCC primary school in Park Walk, at the World's End end of the King's Road.

My father had read that left-wing intellectuals were deluding themselves if they thought they were avoiding the iniquities of the class-ridden English school system by sending their children to the French school in Kensington. The day he read the article was the day he withdrew *les deux petits* and sent my mother to get them places at Park Walk.

My mother says the headmaster was very concerned, and went to great lengths to explain the type of children who attended the school.

'Did you notice the parents who left my office just before you entered?' he had asked her, in lowered tones. 'The father has just got out of prison.'

At this point in the telling, my mother used to leave a pause for the stunned silence that she seemed sure would follow such a shocking revelation.

I think of the moment Magwitch appears in the mist in the opening scenes of

David Lean's *Great Expectations*, and really think that for my mother that day the headmaster's information was a shock on a par with encountering a convict on the Kent marshes.

Bernard Cheeseman was one of the Park Walk boys who, for years, had a flower barrow on the King's Road and would greet my mother with enormous warmth.

'Bernard, you're a pal,' she'd say, as he'd slip her an extra few stems.

They both knew a lot about flowers, and could and would discuss the impact of frost, for example, for what seemed like far too long to me.

I used to listen to them like two characters in a sort of *Cries of London* scene, and was glad he seemed to like my mother, as he looked and sounded like a tough nut to me.

He had a scar, like he'd been slashed by a knife or broken bottle, but it was the result of a rat bite. When he was a child he told my mother that a rat had bitten him when he was a baby in his pram.

He sometimes played with my brother, who instigated gladiatorial games in the school playground at World's End.

Bernard Cheeseman once famously said to my brother – and this is the punch-line – 'I don't like you, but I like your mum!'

32

'As soon as you have a story, you're not being real,' says the blonde, blue-eyed master, staring out from a YouTube video.

I am looking up the reason so many move to Edmonton, Canada, including my brother. I have no sympathy for the teachings of this preacher, and yet, whatever gets you through the night.

John Lennon's line sings through my head: *'It's all right, it's all right.'*

But, actually, is it?

I am struggling with my tendency to piss on the brother's parade (when really it's his own damn business). My mind, which is a bit of a mess, is so full of stories that I can fully admit I am not real to a person such as blonde John of Edmonton. And so, he does not need to be real to me either.

All this choosing of reality and buggering about with its meaning is doing my head in.

I conclude that I am in a fugue, and not the musical sort. I look up the word that came to me as the best way of identifying my present state and see that I might be over-egging the situation. I haven't woken up in New Jersey not knowing how I got there, but I have been wondering how I got to where I am, and why I seem to have forgotten so many touchstones.

I am hooked to the dirt dished on this self-elected holy man and find he has an answer to the anomaly of his own story.

While preaching a vanilla strain of monogamy and fidelity, he is able to file his abuse of two young women, daughters of devotees, under something he calls a 'calling'.

I think of Krishnamurti, and how he was able to brush his own proclivities under a very esoteric rug while all his devotees turned their minds to the great nothing of his instruction.

I heard him pontificating, like a pompous Edwardian, when I was a moody girl, and found his terse points, which all seemed to end with 'Sir', caused me fits of giggles that did not go down well with Alan, the lodger who tried to help me understand fugues of both sorts.

He gave up on me musically, but not in other ways, and told me about making LSD at Oxford when he was working on a chemistry PhD that began to mean less and less to him.

His great love was music. He had toured India as a boy with ENSA, accompanying his father's choir of Welsh miners. He was a brilliant, strange friend of my life, and I love the fact that he left me a painting of himself as a young man, which now hangs in my mother's room.

Yesterday she remarked that he had gone blind, and that it saddened her to see him without his sight. It was a play of light, and so, having adjusted the lighting, I said: 'He can see again now.'

He did go to the Royal College of Music and became a professor there, and also a teacher at Brockwood, Krishnamurti's school in Hampshire.

He first became interested in 'K,' as the inner circle called their unleader, through my father, who was attracted to the man who denied being a deity and who asked *not* to be followed.

I remember my father telling me about him, and so I was keen to attend his talks, but never warmed to K. I called him Special K, like the breakfast cereal, and irritated my dear friend Alan with my flippancy and facetiousness.

I cooled even further when I discovered Krishnamurti did not acknowledge homosexuality, which must have caused Alan deep anxiety.

I much preferred Douglas Harding and his gentle teaching on headlessness. Of course, seeing Alan at the end of a paper bag caused me more convulsive laughter at age 15 than many things.

'What can you see?' said Alan, in a terse tone.

'You, Alan.'

'What else?'

'Nothing.'

In this simple way, you find out you have no head.

Alan was a dear guide of my life. I think of the help he gave me, and how irritable he was with me the night he died. I had brought some elegant soap and he remarked it was the soap that his dear friend María Donska* had always used.

I said: 'That is wonderful.'

'That is not wonderful,' he said sternly, sounding very Welsh. 'I will tell you something that is wonderful, I have been on the phone to the man I have loved with all my heart for twenty years, and he told me that he has always loved me.'

It was a love that the orthodox would call *unrequited*, because it was never reciprocated in any romantic or physical way. The beloved other was a heterosexual. Somehow this moved me deeply.

I told Alan it was 'a brave and beautiful love', when he asked if I thought it was sad.

He asked me if I was sad to say goodbye, and I said it wasn't all about me, which made him smile. And then I added that I was happy for him, and he liked that.

I messed it up a bit by saying that I had always loved him. 'You can go now,' he said, still sounding very Welsh.

And those were the last words he ever said to me in life, but I hear his voice often.

He only liked one bit of my house: a white painting with pipes by Natasha Kidd. It hangs to one side of a window, facing an empty wall with real pipes.

'It has space,' he said.

33

Today it is snowing again, as my mother said it would, and Bonzo doesn't like it so I haven't got my picture of a white snowflake on black fur.

I will write about nothing, and how, some years ago, I had a dream of a dead friend looking dark and brightly alive in a red check shirt. I laughed with delight and hugged him till I realised he was dead, and said:

'Oh no, you're dead.'

I was near to tears and he laughed. 'It's nothing,' he said.

The next day I went to Alan's memorial, where I knew many communities would meet, and so I prepared a few words on *all our Alans* and was followed by a very lovely man who represented the Krishnamurti Foundation.

He said that often 'K' would ask a person what was most important to them. People found it surprisingly hard to answer, so he, Krishnamurti, would tell them that, for him, the answer was *nothing*.

I nearly leapt from my seat because I felt my dead friend had given me the answer in my dreams. Or had I known it all along and chosen the Joe in me to bring it to my attention? I felt like someone who dreams the name of a Derby winner.

Caught between revelations and a more secular interpretation of dreams, I think of rejuvenated Joe saying: 'It's nothing, Marcie,' and making me smile through the mortal shock.

I also think of the Hindi-Catholic ashram where my brother once lived, and how that touched me as holy, and somehow proper.

Also, Rupert Sheldrake★ had been there. Morphic resonance was a relief, and still is. A way to allow the mystery of coincidence, telepathy and the unspoken, without the gobbledygook of a certain New Age certainty.

'It's the height of arrogance,' said Jem, rather grandly, on hearing someone deny extraterrestrial life.

I, too, am wary of demystifiers. Mystery is surely one of the good bits about being here at all.

Yesterday's irritation with gurus was mostly an insane fury with those who preach what they do not practice.

Buddhists and Quakers seem to do things better, but it's not for nothing that my hackles rise. I think again of my brother and Alan as having far more expanded minds than those of their chosen teachers.

I was appalled by Alan having been taken in by EST; not that it didn't offer some obvious insights, alerting all of us, drowning and waving, to the bleeding obvious.

Nothing lasts forever; being in the present is the only time you will be alive.

I paraphrase.

Most programming is junk. Breaking free from societal, parental expectations — if not resonant with your own desires — is vital. The secret is there is no secret.

Agreed.

I always remember a point about libido: 'When you're hot, you're hot; when you're not, you're not.'

I remember 'Wake up Marsha'.

And also, when I went to get my money back, being asked by a tough female trainer what it was like to be 'Marsha all alone'. I didn't really know how to answer that, and thought she might have glimpsed, though my eyes, the real me darting behind a screen.

It was her ability to catch my eye, and keep it for far too long, that got me imagining she'd seen what I myself was looking for, *The Real Me*.

Nobody was meant to speak to each other during coffee breaks, but I said hello to a woman in MacDonald's, and asked: 'Do you come here often?'

She was a curly-haired, pretty woman in her thirties, who was happy to disobey the no-talking rule. We asked each other how we came to be on the course. I said I had been given the training by an EST graduate, a pianist who lived in my mother's house in Chelsea, who wanted to help me.

It turned out it was a last resort for her, she was being denied access to her children.

She had had a brief affair, for which her husband had punished her by keeping the children, and turning them against her.

I was enraged with this unknown husband, and was cursing all men, when one came up and reminded us, in the weediest voice, that we were not supposed to be talking.

I roared out laughing as I thought it was a good joke, and because he had a voice I recognised from Monty Python, but he was really for real.

Suddenly I didn't know what to do with my own weird privilege apart from fall back on my most in-bred, programmed response to anything unfamiliar, and certainly less fortunate: politeness. In those days I would have considered my training condescending and would have avoided speaking to a man, let alone one considerably older than myself, with the welcoming voice of a missionary.

But I made an exception – 'Yes, of course' – when he asked if he might join us ladies. He sold fine cotton at Liberty's.

'Liberty lawns are so fine,' said I, who had something to say on all subjects.

Later, in one of the more brutal sessions, the fabric salesman got up and spoke of a history of sexual abuse, an addiction to hardcore pornography, and a desire to murder women. He had clearly not been vetted carefully, or at all, because he was taken out after howling like a beast and confessing that he 'was not cured', and that earlier that day he had been overcome with murderous intentions towards 'two slags in MacDonald's'.

The pretty woman got told she was old, and no one would ever desire her again. 'Who would want to fuck you?' the trainer yelled. She burst into the floods of tears she clearly needed to release and, by the end of the course ,was through the worst of the fear that she had never mentioned.

She had come to the training believing the version her husband had impressed upon her. He had left her believing she was utterly undesirable. Being told she was not fuckable probably got her over the worst. I could see that she left looking much better.

I said: 'No one is going to fuck with you now,' and we hooted.

I wonder what happened to her. She was a journalist and would be about 75 now.

I learned to understand my own projections and those of others, not that I could always control the projector so well, but it was another clue.

Once, when a teenage daughter was haranguing me for some crime or other, I said: 'Take your movie elsewhere,' and swam off. We were at sea. It became a bit of a catchphrase and came back at me rather often.

I must stop writing now as I want to visit my mother and tell her she was right about there being more snow to come.

I think of the movie *The Last Picture Show*. I'd love to see that again. I haven't seen it since it came out in 1971 and my mother and Imre spoke loudly throughout because he couldn't hear, so my mother explained what was happening and repeated the dialogue. She was always loudly minimal in her descriptions.

He once asked what James Bond was doing outside a window in *Diamonds Are Forever* and she said: 'Just showing off.'

Despite going with the two most embarrassing of companions, I loved *The Last Picture Show*.

My mother's picture-house is closing. There are so many re-runs and she cannot control the projector.

I ask my mother, who has given up on TV, if there is anything she would like to see, and she says *Pygmalion*, with Leslie Howard and Wendy Hiller. I am struck by all sorts of resonances but have no time now to write of flower girls and cut-glass diction this minute.

Maybe tomorrow.

34 *HERRING*

I said to Jem recently that some people thought I had a problem with authority. 'I'm sorry to hear that,' he said, as if I had mentioned mislaying a sock.

I see a photograph of my father by my mother's bed.

'They thought I was lonely and that he would cheer me up.' She laughs, and says again: 'Pissy Farquhar, they called him. After he relieved himself in front of Fleet Air Arm dignitaries.'

I look at this photo of a young man in Fleet Air Arm uniform and I see no one I know, but I like the face, with its slightly supercilious smile.

I think of how I romanced my father's badness and of hearing The Slickers' *Johnny Too Bad,* way after his death, and adding that to my collection of John songs.

He used to like *Big Bad John,* which my mother and I heard on Children's Favourites and sang to him.

'….and you never gave no lip to big bad John.'

He doesn't say much. By the end of the song big bad John is a hero, dead at the bottom of the pit, having saved everyone else, so becomes big *big* John.

I look at a small square photograph I have of a tall thin man, in a hammock in Trinidad, and think *pretty fly.*

A curious thing happens as I think about my 50-year romance with a dead man. I get the sense I have nothing to write that isn't just of my own invention.

Then I look about where I am sitting and see a ledger sticking out from the bookshelf. It's one of the few that escaped the cull. I was drawn to it on account of a strange tale of a dead herring giving my father the will to live, and the fact that at least six pages had been torn out.

Today I read from it, and there they are, thoughts on illness, ageing, and mortality. If this was fiction I'd be drummed out of Creative Writing 101. But it's the real deal, an odd turn up of non-fiction. As I am writing about ageing, and pushing 60, so was he.

He mentions Gilgamesh, Sisyphus and Jesus. I open a page at a note on Krishnamurti reminding him about nothing, and I gasp.

I did feel, when I was clearing my mother's flat, that I was losing her and finding him. He wasn't all bad.

Here's the story I read today:

12 July 1965

The operation and its aftermath were far worse than anyone expected.

Before it fades in my memory, I must put down what seems a turning point in my recovery.

I think it was about three days after the operation. I was allowed into the bathroom and caught sight of myself for the first time in the large glass there. From my appearance it seemed impossible to me that I could actually be alive. My face was drawn and grey and my neck had been replaced by a horrible black bulging bag, hanging straight from my jawbone and disappearing into a collar of blood-soaked dressings taped around my neck, stuck to my shoulders. But my chest, under the bloody collar, was the most horrible sight.

It was a corpse-like, gangrenous green colour, covered from shoulder to waist with bruises which were literally black and blue.

It seemed to be emaciated, with the bruised ribs sticking out. And there were trickles of dried blood down it, all over.

I studied this miserable creature for some time, quite dispassionately and impersonally, and then I thought: 'You poor thing, you haven't much more to offer.'

This thought was without self-pity; it was really an abstract thought and I have no clear idea of its meaning.

Later that evening my supper was brought in and it consisted of a very neatly-filleted and well-cooked whole herring, head, tail and all.

I looked at it and its little filleted ribcage in some way reminded me of my own emaciated, bruised and bloodied chest.

I looked steadily at the herring, and suddenly its small body seemed to speak to me.

'I hope you think I look good,' it said. 'Am I not well-filleted and well-cooked? My body is all that I can give you. I hope you will eat me with pleasure, and that I will make you well and strong. I should be so sad and disappointed if you did not like me.'

The bathos of the poor little sacrificial body struck me suddenly, and tears streamed from my eyes. I ate the little herring completely, leaving nothing, so as not to hurt its feelings. I had to stop between mouthfuls to mop my streaming eyes.

From that moment I think that I began to live again.

But he wasn't all good.

I wrote in episode 7 of a train station farewell, and how my father wished my brother under a wave. They never met again. One of the last things he said, father to son:

'You are the type to go to California and invent a religion.'

It was said with contempt, although I asked my mother: '*Can* you invent a religion?'

I think of a meeting my mother and I attended in Hampstead. It was at the time my brother was in Wisconsin, following a course in miracles, and he had urged us to attend a meeting of his people.

A fat man of at least 60, with a Bisto-rinsed puff of thinning hair, rampaged up and down the aisle of a meeting hall. He was known as 'Dear One.' My mother called him 'Dear boy', as in 'Dear boy is putting himself to a lot of trouble.'

She said: 'He'd be lost without all these middle-aged women.'

I looked about and there *were* a great deal of women in their late forties, all in girlish hippy clothes and thin as sticks. I didn't spot any flesh, and certainly no lipstick.

'What a poor, drab lot,' announced my mother. I replied: 'Please be quiet.' 'Oh,' she said, 'don't worry, they only have ears and eyes for Dear boy.'

She had a point. They punctuated all his exhortations with 'Thank you Lord,' the arms of the faithful arched up to the heavens, shivering in ecstasy.

My mother said: 'Christ!' and I laughed.

There was an invitation to join the ecstasy which, when approached, my mother refused with: 'No thank you, my dear.

One boy, who fell to the floor writhing in the charisma, caught my mother's eye. 'Would you look at that one?' says she, to me.

I needed to go to the lavatory and my mother said she'd enjoy a break. As we passed the gyrating figures crying out: 'Thank you Lord,' my mother paused by the boy who had caught her eye.

'Did you train at RADA?' she asked him. She really did say that.

35

I'm on a train and looking out of the window, appreciating how great it is to have the wide, snowy field to gaze upon without having to look at anything in particular, or press *heart*.

Yesterday I read out a curious story about a well-filleted herring and my father. I noticed no one liked it.

The hardback notebook, with its tiny neat handwriting, is on my mind, but I left it on the floor in the milk-corner. In case anyone is following, the cheese fell through the radiator, hard and contracted.

My mother was silent yesterday.

'How very interesting,' she said once, in a distant, Windsorified voice, frozen in fifties time. It was in answer to a question about the flowers.

Not even the flowers. Not even *Pygmalion*.

'*Pygmalion* came with Leslie Howard and Wendy Hiller.'

Not a flicker in her eyes to suggest anyone at home.

I paint my mother's nails. I wonder if the new peach will be the last colour, then take it off and go back to pink, dusty pink, and say: 'That's better.' To nobody, because my mother isn't listening.

I have changed the hearing aid batteries. The audiologist said: 'She *can* hear you; she is just not listening.'

I look at her *and* see her. She is rehearsing.

My cousin, the famous clairvoyant, brings gifts in shiny puce paper. My mother looks straight through them and I say: 'We will keep them till Christmas.'

I wonder if she'll wait to see another one.

Dr Kroker, the aptly-named gerontologist, sent her home to end her days and the soothsayers said 'by Christmas', but that was well over a year ago.

How many more?

I don't ask Sosostris and she doesn't offer a date. I think of my father saved by a dead herring.

He reckoned he had ten more years in which to make a change in his life; he had less than two. He wanted to be a philosopher-physicist. *He* wanted to invent a religion. The writing is there between the lines.

Daddy – as I never called you – even I can see that insults inflicted on others reveal our own repressed longings.

Do I want to get away with a lack of subtlety on a world stage? Do I envy the bizarre entitlement of Boris Johnson? Do I want to get away with horrible humour and have so many press *heart* on my fat white privilege?

Fuck, I hope not.

I have left my father's book, the ledger, at home. It is on my mind. A draft letter to Imre, apologising for having been very rude, came as a surprise. My father writes contritely but adds he thought he 'could have died from anger.'

I laugh, as I might write such a letter of apology. 'Forgive me for my inexcusable rudeness, but you made me so furious I could have died.'

He tells Imre he is sorry, given that he agrees in principle, with at least 90% of what he was saying, but referring to the bone of contention in a severe tone, my father explains he cannot accept an unprovable point made with such raging assurance.

My father rubs in that Imre's bullying neither wins the argument nor makes it desirable for him to be with him in the same place. Ever again.

He tells him what pills he left the room to take and says, without them, he would have died.

I think it must have been an impossible apology to receive. I notice it was written in the middle of April 1967.

It is clear that the difference of opinion over which my father nearly loses his life concerns the soul or spirit, to which I assume my father was partial, and know that

Imre was not. I remember that when I went to announce my new-found atheism, after seeing *A Clockwork Orange* in 1972, Imre was not so convinced:

'But for little Marsha there will always be the soul.'

'I didn't know I had to give up the soul,' I said, and gave up atheism, which I always found too certain anyway.

Not so long ago I goaded a soul-denier with: 'What do you people have then, a long night of the personality?' I never got an answer.

The six missing pages are the entries that led up to my father's death, three months after the draft letter.

There are a few more notes, after the draft letter, on mortality and suffering, and how weird that people would want to worship a spiteful god. And many other notes towards a leaderless Laozi life. ★

I think how the problematic Irish joke becomes existential wisdom for me – *Follow me, I'll be right behind you* – and how much I love that.

I see how I am my father's daughter, and my mother's too. What would I have been, had I been given away?

I can see the advantage in having been raised by this mysterious woman. I have talked about losing her, but I wonder if I ever found her.

She burned all her diaries after I looked up my birthday and objected to 'A tiring day, the baby (girl) born 8.20.'

I compared it with the joyous raptures she wrote about on encountering my brother, twelve years earlier, and complained.

Ever since my complaint she has revised the memory of the 7th Jan 1958 so that it celebrates the birth of the most beautiful baby ever.

36

Adrian Howells is in my dream, standing. I'm sitting and we are holding hands. It's another 'But you're dead' dream.

Adrian doesn't say: 'It's nothing,' but smiles a sweet *so what*.

I get very agitated because I can feel his hand. I can still feel it as I wake and realise it's my own hand squeezing itself.

I wake and think of angels.

When I was ten, my friend's mother made angels to give to all the children. It is my angel still, and I think about it and how it comes out year after year.

About twenty years ago, she gave me a new, improved one, with a polystyrene ball for a head, but I much preferred the one with a ping pong ball head. My angel will be 50 next year.

4 years ago, I got the following text from Adrian:

Clarence, u were the wind beneath MY wings as well as your own Tuesday pm! It was totally gorge-of-the-arses to see u and I honestly LOVED our time together and your emphatic company and conversation was JUST what the consultant psychiatrist would have ordered! Today has been a cheese sandwich kinda day, thank God! Who knew??!! SOO much love to u! Adrian xxx PS I've started an online petition to secure Olive first dibs as the Angel Gabriel for next year's nativity!

When I first started the *Pushing 60* chronicles, back in 2014, I mentioned cheering someone up. He had no name back then, in case he didn't want strangers knowing of his sadness.

We had tea in December 2013, and I made him laugh, telling him how his friend

Stewart Laing and I had been unappreciated by a critic. Her sure little words – 'neither clever nor funny' – had struck me a blow of unprecedented upset, probably because it was the night Ella was giving birth and I was feeling more deep and doubtful than clever *or* funny.

I looked her up to find she had written the biography of a very clever and funny man.

I saw pictures on my phone, of a neat and tidy woman, and thought of Stewart Laing, Adrian Howells, and Leigh Bowery, and how I'd rather be rolling up and down their aisles any day, than failing to be good company for the phallic biographer.

As luck would have it, I saw the arbiter of taste at a cash machine in Kentish Town railing against her companion, a tall hapless-looking man, the sort that often gets called a decent bloke. Of course, one never knows.

When I told Adrian, I gave a dramatic urgency and comedic force to the occasion which the real incident had lacked. I think 'neither clever nor funny' came out from under my breath as I caught her eye for the briefest flash.

In the version that cheered us up, which I have now forgotten, my part was way more audible, heroic: the three little words projected, not muttered. Heroic and massively more amusing.

Adrian and I met that day in a toy shop. I had just heard the news that Olive, my granddaughter, had been robbed of her chance to be a donkey in the nativity play. I told Adrian that the poor child was inconsolable and hated being a townsperson. She had been so proud of her part as a donkey. We assumed she was demoted because of arsey behaviour, which Adrian and I agreed was a perfect disposition for the donkey, an ass by any other name.

When Olive was born, 3 months early, she lived in an incubator in Govan for what seemed an eternity. Adrian gave me the most wonderful support. His art and life was full of a love that was real, and that is something marvellous. I still wish he had been as kind to himself as he was to others.

Another point in his text that catches my eye, and clutches my heart, is the

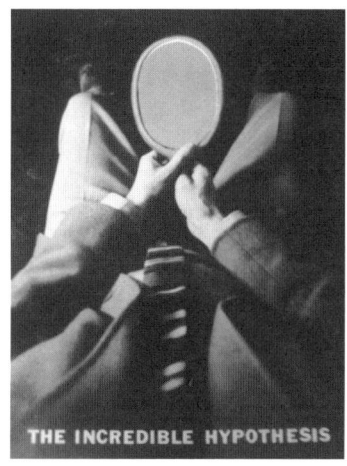

31. *Brownie* 1966; 32. Douglas Harding, *Headlessness* 1972; 33. *Projector*, 36. *neither clever nor funny*, Salon project by Stewart Laing, 2013; 35. *Torn out pages*, sometime in the late sixties; 34. *Father's notes on a Herring*, 1965.

reference to cheese sandwiches. I told him my recollection that Camus had said how it was often a choice between suicide and a cheese sandwich, and, as someone who believed in being happy despite the utter bleakness, he opted for the latter.

When I mentioned this to Adrian's dearest friend after his death, she said he'd 'maybe just got fed up with cheese sandwiches,' and that made me smile, and weep.

Now I am here in Glasgow for the first time since my last tea with Adrian.

I am in a rush as I must add finishing touches to my one-time-only, one-woman Christmas show: *Call Me Ivy*, which opens and closes tonight at the wonderful CCA, and is dedicated to the truly wonderful Adrian Howells.

37

I am on another train, the return of the vaudevillian.

I reminded everyone that I was not an actor last night, as with all my force I channelled Big Marcia, my aunt, as I shimmied down an imaginary staircase (or rather, a spiralling pine stairway) and threw up my hands, as Adrian Howells, exclaiming:

'I don't believe it! What did she say?!'

This exclamation goes with a tale of a black rubber bath hat which has a slightly padded rubber stalk on top. To some, the stump on top, and the material, caused this bath hat to exude a whiff of S&M. To me it was a bath hat of elegant surreality.

It was for this reason I put it on my mother, one not-so-long-ago Christmas.

I have explained that I think the open door is the only door in this peculiar season, and I have also said that those at loose ends are often much better company than one's own flesh and blood, so it's a win-win situation.

One way to give the anyone and anybodies of such gatherings a way to make collective sense of each other is to suggest a theme.

One year it was 'Surreal Christmas' and, not wanting to put my mother to any bother, I put the rubber beret with a stalk on her head. She looked supremely surreal.

One guest we never saw again grew a full beard with moustache and shaved half of it off.

I could wander back with ease to all the ingenious interpretations, but must get to the punchline.

When Adrian Howells saw the noirish beret, it was as my bath hat, hanging in my daughter Ella's bathroom in Glasgow.

'*Whose* is that?'

'It's Marcia's,' said Ella, 'she made my grandmother wear it last Christmas.'

'I don't believe it! What did she say?!'

'Ask Marcia.'

He appeared, holding the beret bath hat.

'Your mother wore this?!' he exclaimed, in most exaggerated tones of amazement.

'Yes,' said I, nothing else to say.

'What did she say?'

'Nothing,' said I.

'But how did she feel about it?'

I said: 'Fine, she was happy to be alive.'

At this he doubled up in contortions of mirth.

I hadn't meant to be funny, but I can see the funny side now.

Last night I heard a hearty laugh from the front row of the fairy-lit dark. It was a beautiful young man, another dear student of Adrian's.

I am wondering about names. I have caused so much unwitting hilarity with some of my anonymising that maybe I should just call the young man David.

In 1999, to protect my husband's privacy, I gave him the name Keith, just because someone once, who never remembered names, called him Keith. This caused shrieks of laughter, way back in the nineties, in The South London Gallery.

Only when I heard the laughter did I realise why they thought it funny I had given my husband the name of the most hip and happening, *truly Scottish* Farquhar in the art world.

I like to be in on the jokes I make.

What's in a name?

A lot.

Lot, for example. I think of that name, and particularly his wife, who famously looked back.

What's all this to-ing and fro-ing? Onwards.

Great Wikipedia entry, by the way: *Spouse: Lot. Died: Sodom.*

One Christmas, my brother and I were driven by a very cheerful young woman called Meldy to Eel Pie Island.

Eel Pie Island was famous in the sixties for rock'n'roll parties that lasted for days and lived on in the imagination of people like myself, who were not there.

By the time of our Christmas visit, in the early seventies, the island was an estate agent's dream of a safe and exciting place to be. Safe and exciting not being adjectives that go together, unless you happen to be a city boy, which is what my cousin was.

It was clear, on the long drive out to the island, that Meldy was most enamoured of cousin Patrick.

My mother, who was sitting in the front, was a good listener to the love-struck driver, who was so excited to be spending Christmas with Pat's family.

We called him Patrick.

My brother and I sat in the back seat, giggling at nothing like twats. He was 27 but not quite right in the head, and I was 15 and not quite all there myself. Our mother made a good impression for all of us.

When we arrived at the island the oddness began.

Our cousin's riverside *des res* could have been in any dully affluent suburb. Not the faintest trace of rock'n'roll mayhem anywhere. It was immediately and sadly apparent that there was no excitement of any sort, and our cousin was not in the least interested in Meldy. Well, not in *that* way.

Our uncle, who was a very kind man, offered us all drinks and we sat in a festive silence, a silence full of my mother's cheery observations regarding the decorations, delicious smells, our enjoyable drive and, of course, the constant giggling from the brother and me.

Pat, as we now knew him, was in the kitchen having refused Meldy's help. Another bad sign, as any eager suitor would surely have leaped at the chance to be alone basting a turkey with the desirable other?

Nobody asked where my bi-polar aunt happened to be, as there are some questions you do not ask...

After a considerable length of time, which might have been twenty minutes, we all heard an entrance being made at the top of a spiralling pine staircase. From on high, my aunt, in a red velour housecoat trimmed with cotton wool, began her descent with a large glass in one hand, teetering on perilous mules.

My mother said: 'Christ', out loud. The shock had slipped out involuntarily at first sight of her big sister.

Once in the room, my aunt made a beeline for Meldy.

'You must be the darling girl.'

Meldy said: 'I'm Meldy.'

'*Yes,* darling Meldy,' said my aunt.

'I am very pleased to be here, and to meet you,' said Meldy, actually looking shyly thrilled.

'Are you darling?' said my aunt. 'You adorable girl.'

And with that, she unzipped her housecoat a little bit further and plunged Meldy's face into her ample cleavage as she uttered the unforgettable words:

'Welcome to the bosom of the family.'

'Christ,' said my mother.

'Anyone for a top-up?' said my uncle.

My brother and I giggled.

'Is mum down?' called Pat from the kitchen.

Last night I trimmed a red velour housecoat with cotton wool and welcomed the audience.

A blonde-haired pretty face mask, worn on the back of my head, went down well, a cheap and attractive way to be Janus.

I certainly offered ways to make something out of nothing. With pinking shears, a hole puncher, and old Christmas cards, glue and glitter, you need never have to buy another tag.

The audience had gone when I found the lost cork which I singed. After drawing a curly moustache and goatee on my face, I left the artist's apartment and went off into an icy night with David.

This morning I pulled gold paint out of my black rubber washbag instead of toothpaste. In the semi-dark of a country morning, I nearly squeezed it onto my brush.

The critic smiles.

38 OB-LA-DI, OB-LA-DA

Ob-la-di, Ob-la-da...

Jimmy Scott thought he should have got the credit for the song.

'But it's just an expression,' said Paul McCartney.

Irony of the most blatant type, getting het up about such a line.

I totally get it. Life in a nutshell.

I am trying not to groan on a tube train

I did let out a deep throat howl last week and frightened a man lost in thought. I apologised, as he might have mistaken my lumbago cry as a warm-up to something more immediately dangerous to his person.

The pain makes me direct; I ask how long it takes to get a body off the tracks.

The young steward on the indefinitely-stalled train last night was appalled at the casual cruelty in my enquiry. He said something about it being a life, someone's life.

If this were old-fashioned fiction, the impatient traveller with lumbago who has no time for unknown suicides will later learn it is her own son on the line, or herself, if there is a time warp element.

Tonight I will dance in my flamenco tartan dress, which hasn't been out since the year before last, and might not even fit.

I am so tired, and my back is very sore.

Every year I do my pissed aunt at Christmas turn at Cabaret Melancolique. I missed last year, but the idea is it's the annual tired routine, brought out with a stamp of defiance (and sometimes knickerless) to reflect the Balmorality of all kilt, no drawers. Tonight there will be underwear.

I usually introduce the annual fling with a story of the season. I choose a bleak but ultimately uplifting tale, or that is my intention; I think some find my cheerfulness even more melancholic. So be it. Each to their own.

A great story about buying crackers seems too sad because the beautiful woman I meet in the bookshop has gone, but what the hell, I'll tell it anyway.

Looking For Crackers on Christmas Eve.

After one of my daughters had called the boyfriend of the other daughter 'DEATH', and told him to leave the house immediately, I said: 'Come back in the spring; we're better at Easter.'

I then went out with the name-calling daughter, Kitty who had been most upset at the thought she was going to have to share the festivities with Death, on a search for crackers. As we got more and more desperate to find these must-have-items, their name seemed to become more and more apt, more and more absurdly fitting.

Kitty saw a man carrying some and ran a great distance at very high speed like an ostrich. When he crossed the road, so did she, and finally caught him only to hear him say he had got the last box.

We went into a bookshop, where I thought we might get wrapping paper and make our own silent variety. We bumped into the mother of a friend of Kitty's, a very sensitive, beautiful woman, who asked me how I was. That is when I told her, giving her an unexpurgated account of Kitty's response to our visitor.

'Yes, she called him "Death" we can't get crackers, and I am done in. I can't bear it a minute longer and it hasn't even begun…'

'I am so sorry,' I said, at the end of my endless spew of seasonal wretchedness.

'No, you have cheered me up, you're so sane,' she said, and called after me, as I was walking down the street, 'I love you.'

'I love you too!' I called back.

We were planning to see more of each other and compare notes on adult daughters and ancient mothers, and we never did, because she died.

Here's a tip: seize the day, any old day, to be in touch. It used to be a BT slogan, now it just seems vital.

This is the season of ghosts, of course.

The year before last an artist I know, representing Death at the Cabaret, pointed at me. I raised my glass to him, the Grim Reaper, because I didn't know what else to do. *Ob-la-di, Ob-la-da.*

39 *STEPS*

I loved that film of derring-do in Scotland, and, of course, the genius of the twist. I want to see it again. I want to write out the wonder of it here, but might spoil it for someone who needs a tip for an old movie to watch.

Oh, Mr Memory, what a character, what an act, and what a great name, which I borrowed way back for a performance lecture in Cork on the vagaries of recall.

Miss Memory, I called myself, and got a very kind mention in an Irish art journal, which pleased my mother. It was something she kept, and which I took with me from her souvenirs of a lifetime.

Two years ago yesterday she took the last steps she would ever take .

It's got a good old-fashioned story, and Robert Donat is a perfect Hannay as far as I remember, which isn't that far some days.

I have *Pygmalion* with Leslie Howard to take to watch with Mother, but I think *The 39 Steps* would be another perfect treat.

When Jem and I first met, on a teaching English to foreigners course, he was a photographer. Shanne Bradley remembers that when she first met Jem at their squat in Burton Street, she was relieved to see an Andy Warhol Factory type.

He took a beautiful photograph of the clock-tower of St Pancras station and turned it into a real clock. It was a collaboration, a money-making scheme.

I drew a little Hannay to hang from the minute hand.

The photograph was laminated, the cheap battery-operated clock mechanism attached at the back, with the hands showing on the clock face.

Jem's friend was doing a market stall at the time and said he would sell our five prototypes, but after a few weeks of no sales it was Christmas, so we gave them to our mothers, Jem's father, my aunt Marcia, and we kept one.

My mother was delighted and praised the photograph and the ingenuity of the design.

On Boxing Day, I asked her if the little man had fallen off, and she said: 'Oh no, I took that off, as it spoiled it.' I laughed and said: 'That was my bit.' 'Well,' she said, 'it's better without it.'

She kept that figureless, hand-free, grease-splattered, wipe-clean clock for all those years. I took that home, too.

I wonder what is going to become of the cumulative sentimentality of my own stuff when the time comes to throw it all away.

I wonder about sparing the future and doing it myself, and then think on the bittersweet jolts I got from each and every saved drawing and handmade card. I never knew she cared.

On the subject of steps, I missed one last night and landed in a pratfall to rapturous applause. I made it look effortless. Well, an accident is effortless. My knee is bruised and tender and my funny bone is in pain. The lumbar regions are tender and I am off to do it again tonight.

I didn't tell the crackers story, but I did tell an extended version of the *ob-la-di* one.

Last Christmas was bleak, as I had failed in my effort to keep my mother at home and she knew she was going to *a home*.

She rang her bell at night to tell me that she was sorry to be a burden and how everybody would be so much better once she had been put away. I was torn to shreds by the nightly guilt trips and hid in corners of my brain where I was running over poppy fields with my dog.

Of course, at this point Bonzo was a pooing and peeing puppy who was not even allowed to put his paws on the pavement. He stayed with me those long nights and my mother called him my boyfriend. I could hear her ask the carers, rather bestially, if Marcia was with her boyfriend.

I used him as a way in to her affections, and it worked.

'You understand,' she would say to him, and he certainly looked as if he did.

The other irresistible force was Sammy the baby, who caused my mother to sing *Patsy Fagan*.

'*You're a harum, scarem, divil may carem, decent Irish boy!*'

He certainly looked like one, with his very dark hair and big blue eyes.

Without the baby and the dog there was no end to the sadness and anger in the room.

I have written a great deal about this, and the sense of being profoundly alone in the living presence of my mother. But in answer to the question I ask myself – who are you telling? – the only answer seems to be myself. I am telling myself.

The farmer wants a wife, hey ho janierio, the farmer wants a dog.

My mother sang that country ballad beautifully yesterday, with the farmer wanting everything: a baby, a nurse, a bone.

It makes total sense. Her distant friendliness is a miracle after last year and, like her, I think I am telling happy stories.

But, back to last year, when she wished me a happy Christmas in a wireless-era voice of public address.

I didn't go into much detail in the four-minute turn last night, but I did say I shared a bottle of champagne with the Christmas Day carer, a friend of a friend.

According to our mutual friend, we met in another life and were extraordinarily successful business men. How dull that sounds. I thought we could at least have been Antony and Cleopatra, but whatever… Mandy was sensitive to the pain. She knew.

I didn't say all this last night, just that we got drinking after a frosty response to my presence from my mother.

I said: 'Ob-la-di, Ob-la-da', and Mandy told me her brother-in-law, Jimmy Scott the conga player, had always said that, and that's how he came to think the Beatles song was his. I could relate to the exquisite nonsense of being infuriated about one's catchphrase being immortalised in someone else's song, but what a line to crave ownership over.

I told that in under a minute, and somehow managed to communicate my fellow feeling for the conga player.

I then put on my Farquhar-tartan flamenco dress which did zip up, after a struggle. Jem said: 'Breathe in,' but when has breathing in ever lessened the size of breasts?

He then played the hurdy-gurdy beautifully. I felt the deep bloodshed of ancient Scotland and danced with gormless gusto to the beat of a wonderful audience.

But when he got going on the Spanish the spirit moved me, the *duende* no less; I felt the breasts rise like bulls' horns. I felt the pain, the agony and ecstasy, welling up and coming through the untutored steps. I cried my own *Ole!* for us all – all women, all men – and all the pain left my lower back. I was in the dance of a lifetime, and then I fell, and the audience roared out their approval.

Brian Catling said he'd never seen me do anything as good. I said: 'It wasn't me.'

40

Jem once played the part of a suitor of my mother's called Pearland Dean in *The Londoners,* an episodic soap opera of life in a Chelsea boarding house.

The gentleman in question answered my grandmother's advertisement for linoleum. In wartime London, lino was scarce.

When he saw the floor-covering was pink, he declined, because it was intended for his office in Wardour Street. My grandmother called my mother.

'Before you go, Mr Dean, you must meet my daughter. Originally the linoleum was in her nursery in Ireland.' Very cunning move on the part of the pink lino-seller.

Charles Dean told me, thirty years later, that the moment he saw my mother was the moment he fell in love, and immediately wrote a cheque for the linoleum.

The still-smitten suitor sat down at a grand piano in a King's Road flat, where we met in the seventies, and said: 'Let me play you something I wrote the first day I saw your mother.'

He sang a sentimental song in the voice of Noël Coward and played the piano with the flourishes of a boy in love. I loved it. I remembered only one phrase:

The pink linoleum that kissed your baby feet…

I wrote a song around that line for Jem to sing in my soap. He brought a Casio and sang it wonderfully while playing the part of Pearland as the ancient boy. I had called the character Pearland Dean because the real-life man about town was Charles Dean, of Pearl and Dean advertising.

Jem got into the part so fully that he exceeded his allotted time and I had to get him off the stage. He made up a spontaneous stick and stumble routine and fell off the stage to roars of approval.

The real Charles Dean got the lino and the girl, for a while at least.

My mother told Kitty not so long ago that she had loved him, but that her mother had put a stop to it.

Kitty was very sympathetic and thought it awful that my grandmother had waited for the love-struck pair one night on the steps of the house in Oakley Street, holding a sword.

Charles had given my mother a sword with their names on it. 'Take your sword, Mr Dean, and be gone.'

I can't remember if we ever heard what more, if anything, the pious mother had to say, but he got the message.

Kitty asked how my mother could have accepted such draconian interference. 'Well,' said my mother, 'he was a bit older.' 'How much older?' asked the curious granddaughter.

'Thirty years,' said my mother, quite dreamily.

'I totally understand your mother now,' said Kitty.

My mother laughed and said: 'I suppose.'

A girl of 18 and a 49-year-old. So thirty *one* years older.

He was a very dapper chap at 80, when he came back into her life.

He sent my mother photographs of himself, one of which has turned up on the side of the fridge. It caught my eye today. I only met him once. He married three times, because, so he told me, he had only ever loved my mother.

'Dreadful man,' said my elderly cousin recently, 'most unsuitable.'

41 *A REAL PAL*

'Some people are absurdly determined to be unreal.'

My brother says this in answer to a story I tell him of relative grief, my term for unsatisfactory communications with distant cousins. At least I have been willing, if not absurdly determined, to be real.

'What is real?' one often hears in less thrilling conversations.

What is normal? What is sane?

What is a fucking dull rhetorical question…

I am lost for words, which is to say there are so many that I am lost *in* them.

My mother said I looked tired today, and that it was probably the pain. She compared lumbago to being in labour,

'Absolutely,' I say, and she says:

'Yes, it will go.'

So I change the batteries in her hearing aids.

She remembers Esmonde* and asks if he has 'gone'.

'Yes.'

'Oh yes, I remember,' she picks up, 'Esmonde went early. He got a taxi from the station, said to the driver he was "going to have a little rest", closed his eyes, and died. The driver said: "Sir, we have arrived," but he got no answer.'

My mother is in a fine storytelling mood. 'Lucky Esmonde,' said I.

'Indeed,' said my mother, and we smiled faintly. 'He used to knock his pipe on his head. Why?' I'm sure she knows, but has closed her eyes.

He used to slide down through the seat of an armchair till only his head and arms seemed to still be on the chair. He was a very curious adult, and we loved him.

When my brother was *recovering*, as it was called, Esmonde, who taught at LSE, would give him articles to type.

My brother, who had been a high-speed, hunt and peck typist from days of routine journalism, nearly died a psychomotor death after the ECT treatments.

Mogodon-slow and sad, he would go and pack china at an exclusive Sloane Street shop, where the mother of the most beautiful girl (the one who called David Bowie boring) worked and gave my brother a break.

Ha! The china theme.

The night of his brainstorm, as my mother called it, he hurled all the cups and plates into the garden. We found china for years afterwards and I glued it together in an early art experiment.

When I was 14, a rather beautiful boy came to visit me and I suggested climbing over some walls to an empty garden. Looking back, of course, he must have thought this was a much better invitation than it turned out to be, because I then asked him to help me find china. There was a lot of broken china in that back garden too

Just as he was about to kiss me, my mother called over the walls, a *yoo-hoo*ing, Enid Blyton-type-call. Most off-putting.

Back to Esmonde.

At this slow time of my brother's, Esmonde would bring papers that spilled about him in the billows of swirling smoke as he explained his thesis and said how much he appreciated my brother's ability to decipher his terrible writing.

Weeks would pass, and Esmonde would come back to receive maybe two pages, which he would greet with enormous delight, and pay my brother. Kindness enough to prick the eyes. I hunt and peck through tears, thinking of this very kind man. I asked my mother at the time if Esmonde was really impressed by my brother's work.

'Of course not,' she had said.

'A real pal' she said, and I like that. I think of real friends, and the real, and how unreal it is all beginning to feel.

When Theresa May announced her alliance with the DUP, I said: 'It is officially a fiction now to be called the made-up party.'

'That's all over the internet,' said a killjoy acquaintance.

But I was glad to know I wasn't the only one who had heard the real message in the fusion.

I asked Jem last night if I am imagining the worst, and he says he has never before feared nuclear war. I am amazed, as I spent my very young years seeing flashes and mushroom clouds in my dreams. I was frightened to go to sleep, and would ask my father about Hiroshima to make it real, so I could get some rest.

Jem says he wasn't aware of it back then.

'You were not aware of CND marches or anything?' I ask him, incredulously. 'Maybe they sheltered you.'

'Yes, they did keep me in a shelter,' he says.

And I laugh and laugh… A real laugh, not to be polite. It's not even that funny; it was the way he said it.

And because it's good to laugh.

I got a card today. It's a monoprint of a red Christmas tree on a green card. The red paint is uneven and some has dripped off the tree, appearing to be red snow. It is signed 'Konrad' in the bottom right.

Inside, it says: 'Konrad didn't like his card and didn't want to take it home. But I like it bloody well. Happy Holidays, see you soon, Mark.'★

Such a funny message. I like it bloody well, too.

Bonzo is barking at mice, and it's cold, sitting still tapping. 'STOP,' I laugh at Bonzo and he looks a bit cross. It's time to go.

42 *LONG*

It was frosty and foxy in Norwood in the middle of the night.

I mention *Pushing 60*, and Katy says she has listened to a couple but can't remember them.

She remembers hearing one about somebody – she can't recall who it was – and thinking: 'Marcia knows a lot of people.'

'Do you remember a number?' I ask. 'Well actually, I'm sorry, I don't.'

'Oh no,' she says, 'Oh dear, I should never have said I'd listened.'

I laugh another good laugh and think of the wonderful relief of a friendship of over 50 years. The great pleasure in getting on is that the tracks are down and, although some have rerouted or are missing, there are others that remain and remind us of the times of our lives, in all their details, and of nothing in particular.

I tell Katy that I wrote about Esmonde Robertson yesterday, and we remember his sister Olivia★ and a ludicrous outing to the river to float a boat.

It was indistinguishable from any other paper boat, save for some hieroglyphs and ankhs drawn across it by Olivia in a hurry, in biro.

Esmonde's sister Olivia was a High Priestess of Isis. She was sympathetic to mental illness as she had been diagnosed herself.

Olivia later knew her visions to be mystic revelations, and that no doctor could cure her of her divinity.

I loved this esoteric visitor when I was a child, she never told me not to show off, nor said I talked too much. She encouraged it all, and took me to Parliament Hill to be a Mabin in a spring ceremony with her friend Ross Nichols, the Druid, in 1968.

She said I had a mystic aura, and when I went to visit her on a working trip with

37. *Surreal Christmas*, 2008. 41 *Broken china;* 38. *Crackers,* 40. *Elderly suitor with Gruffalo.* 42. *Back to back with Olivia.* 39. *Farquhar tartan flamenco,* 1999.

Mark Noll, to look for fairies, she said I still had it.

Mark, who sent Konrad's card yesterday, was very amused, because the first thing Olivia said when she met him was how my mother was so at ease with homosexuality. Mark asked her if she was not.

'Not so much,' she replied, and hooted with mirth.

We all had great fun together because her fondness for fertility, in relation to her mission as a High Priestess of Isis, had never translated into the slightest inclination towards having babies.

Mark and I both noticed her very good-looking followers. There was a noticeboard with bright, young, beautiful people. She said she only chose the pretty ones and was proud to tell us that Mick Jagger was a visitor.

I visited her again in 2007 with Judith Goddard,★ who filmed the occasion. It is clear (and rather sad) how much I revel in the flattery, and the news that my father is so pleased I am there.

In the sixties, my father gave lectures on physics and metaphysics by invitation of Olivia and her other brother, a former Anglican priest, who had transformed the family chapel into a temple.

Olivia loved my father, and I also warmed to her for that reason.

When I last visited her, she told me to tell her a story: 'Do Mathew, do Dermot.'

She had remembered a wedding party where I had performed, singlehandedly, every single guest, just for her. I was Dermot, the penniless, hippy groom, Mathew, the father of the bride — known as Money Bags — and various assorted guests. My solo show made Olivia laugh and laugh back in the late sixties, but I had long forgotten the hippy wedding by 2007.

She said my mother was the best storyteller she had ever known.

I told my mother that on my return, to which the best storyteller replied: 'Does she indeed?' and proceeded to tell a story of how she had received a letter from Olivia in the sixties, saying that my father John was having an affair with an American academic.

My mother wrote back, thanking her for her letter, adding that it was as delightful as ever to have heard from her, and how John always looked so refreshed returning from his visits.

Some years after his death, Olivia came over for an Isis occasion and invited herself to supper. I found my mother pulling grey flesh off a chicken carcass.

'What are you doing?'

'I'm making a fricassee,' said my mother, grandly.

Of course, there were no traditional cooking methods applied to my mother's version of this dish, which often came in a gluey, off-white sauce. I called it a 'frick arse' under my breath.

'Olivia is a vegetarian,' I said.

'Well I won't be handing out the recipe.'

Olivia enjoyed the supper and congratulated my mother on the ingenuity of her vegetarian cooking.

My mother smiled, and hailed her a taxi when the time came. The Priestess blew kisses from the cab window, calling my mother by the most affectionate names. My mother waved widely from the steps, smiling and saying quite audibly:

'Goodbye, you silly old cow.'

Katy and I enjoy this story because we both know, and love, the dark side of impeccable manners, especially those of our mothers.

Much later in the lives of us all, I took my mother to an esoteric afternoon at Swedenborg House, where she received a great welcome and responded like a suffering dignitary.

Afterwards we were invited to a special ceremony for Isis. My mother very reluctantly agreed. I invited Katy.

It was a cold night, and we met in the volunteer-run vegetarian cafe in Bonnington Square, one of the last places in London to have a connection to seventies squatting. Olivia sat beside a long thin man in black who was introduced as a wizard and artist of excruciatingly detailed supernatural pornography.

I was quite unable to buy one of his works, although we were instructed to do so by Olivia, who was in an excitable state as she had decided to ordain a new High Priestess that very night.

Today, Katy and I roar with laughter at the memory of the new High Priestess, a rotund woman in her sixties wearing a belted mac.

'The sort that makes an effort to go to the Chelsea Flower show,' said Katy.

The high priestess elect and my mother made conversation about Penge and Pissarro, and then we went to the river, crossing the wide and lunatic traffic system around the MI5 building, and took some time to find a concrete walkway to the holy Isis by Vauxhall.

We were a very small group: My mother, Olivia, the wizard, Katy and SR, who has come into these chronicles as the person who did not put Nancy Spungen on a plane. My mother complained loudly to SR, who was warming her hands, that I had led her to believe she was going to see a great Nile vessel on the Thames, not a little paper boat.

She kept thanking SR for holding her hands and saying that her kindness was the highlight of the evening. She pretended not to hear the incantations we were asked to repeat and made observations on dull things quite audibly.

At the end, she said: 'Heartiest congratulations, my dear,' to the new High Priestess and thanked Olivia for another 'memorable occasion'.

Katy's niece, Essi, says Thanksgiving is a celebration of genocide and Katy makes a case for the pilgrim fathers being dissenters, refugees themselves, and I say I'm happy that teenagers are thinking otherwise. I am quite amazed at how many brilliant Americans go pumpkin pie-eyed over their turkey holiday.

When I was just five, we learned a religious song at school: *There is a happy land far, far away*, and my brother, then 16, said: 'Sounds great, where is it?'

I only remember this because he said my answer was 'really good'; I had said: 'America.' He said: 'Go and sing your song to John and tell him where the happy land is.'

My father was not amused, and told me terrible things about America ever afterwards. He told me pet shop owners there told lies about goldfish memory just to sell the poor creatures in tiny bowls to the gullible. He told me that they lied about smoking to sell cigarettes and punished great men like Charlie Chaplin. He said they were swindlers, ate too much and that they celebrated cheating the American Indians.

My mother said he exaggerated, and America was a great country that had helped 'us' in the war.

My father called me an American once, all because I wanted a Barbie doll, which I never got.

When he died, the Americans who took me to Billy Graham also took me to see the Black and White Minstrel Show *Over my father's dead body*. My mother said it wasn't her cup of tea.

My American friends had a load of Barbies, and beautiful, big white teeth. They were very kind to me, but I was happier with Katy's family where there were no Barbies.

43

It was frosty and foxy in Norwood in the middle of the night.

I like that line from yesterday, but it never went where I was hoping it might. These daily *writes* of passage are never quite as…

Not all harsh words are unkind. I think of all the little acts-of-kindness initiatives and I have to stop myself from ridiculing them.

I am always banging on about kindness myself.

It's dark now, and almost midwinter. As I have told you before, I once heard a country witch warning quite categorically that spring is not the only season and making a very good case for winter, death itself, the *without whom* of rebirth. No wonder ancients made fire.

A Christmas card comes, from a dear friend I never see, 'with love from fiery California.' Hell on earth, and how.

I am demented by loss and write to SR about it. It's not such beautiful writing or anything but it reflects a melancholy that I actually feel. She writes back so elegantly that I am glad I mentioned the lowlights.

I call myself vain and a beauty therapist disagrees. (Well, she would, wouldn't she?) I'm having a facial and reflexology.

While the cold, gold, gelatinous mask works on my pores, I think of my mother only having been to the hairdresser once in her life, and then stop myself feeling bad by counting breaths.

Katy reminded me that we both grew up surrounded by portraits of our beautiful mothers.

It's true. I have four now. Ella has two. It wasn't my mother's choice; The MacEgan★

was her relation and her grandmother's suitor.

My mother said recently: 'It is very wrong to interfere in the love affairs of a woman in her eighties,' and I agreed.

Apparently, family greed on the part of my grandmother, the daughter-in-law, prevented the marriage between the woman who my mother still calls Granny, and The MacEgan.

I consider my pose at school, the outsider in an art overall.

It was more flattering, blue and wrap-around, and I wore it over underwear so couldn't just take it off. The artist was a good cover.

Of course, The MacEgan was a real artist, and the woman he loved was a fine water-colourist. My mother's grandmother took her paints and walked for miles with the man she loved.

I told my mother when she aired her objection to interfering in love affairs that I always cite her as a great influence, alongside Samuel Beckett.

She said: 'He loved Nola.'

I found a letter from my mother's older sister. It was from just after my parents, the honeymooners – I cannot, and do not need to imagine – had been to see her. This was when she gave my mother a painting of the Kerry Hills.

This is the painting I have now had to move, on account of it having been so often altered by the woman who would appear at night to add a lake that never was. The lake I said I had seen before, but then kept quiet about. I heed the advice not to disagree with dementia sufferers.

In the letter, the much older sister refers to their brother as a 'vapid ass', and says she is trying to recover from the family. She praises my mother for being unlike any of them, and calls her a kind and loving spirit. This sister died young, which is sad because I loved her leprechaun stories and her drawings and the rumour of her astounding intellect and scholarly knowledge of Swift. My mother says I would have loved her, and I think I really would have.

I love how John Calder writes about Samuel Beckett's kindness, and think of others who go about the daily dread, giving what they can without naming the deed.

I remove, from my mother's handbag, a brooch I made her. The circles within the circle are perfectly cut, and the moonstone is beautifully set. It is proof of my care and attention; that I have some tangible skills.

Also attached to the same piece of old cloth are her wings, the Fleet Air Arm sweetheart brooch, the design of which thrills me: wings either side of a nautical anchor. There is something secure and soaring about an anchor between wings.

The last brooch is in the shape of a letter, the first letter of the name of her school in Dublin. The school where she was asked to clear her desk after the other girls had gone home so there would be no embarrassment.

'She was a very fine woman,' says my mother of the headmistress, 'and most dismayed to have to ask me to leave.'

There are many stories of such casual cruelty suffered by my mother, who was one of many to be deprived of an education.

Why all this? And why not?

I have a painting in my bathroom, of a castle besieged by Cromwell. It's by The MacEgan. It was where my mother and her brother went digging for treasure, which they never found. The family forgot about the ruin when they left in impoverished haste. Fifty years later, having reverted to the state, rumour has it Americans bought it, and maybe it's now a family seat of fictional Fenians.

Here's the end of a little penny book by the scholarly and spirited Nola. It is the tale of a boy and a leprechaun, *Paudeen and Zub*.

Paudeen has come back from his adventures with the leprechaun and is exhausted.

His mother carried him to the big bed in the kitchen and laid him gently down. Then she went to the half door and leaned out. It was a beautiful night full of stars and the gurgling of the river.

She thought she heard a silvery sound like laughter in the shadows. Raising her eye to the bright blueness of the early night she muttered: 'Tomorrow night there will be a new moon, that will be a great night for the Leprechauns.'

44

It is becoming so clear that sharing the dread is not to be sneezed at. The brave and bold way of going about *going on* is a real light in all of this. I am touched deeply by the good in people at the moment and see this as the brightest of silver linings.

The beautiful writing I received from two important friends★ makes me relieved to have been honest about the experience of being in the dark.

I feel tears coming up and spilling out in answer to the osteopath's question as to whether my mother was artistic.

I think of all the inventions of my now still mother. I can't write of them now, but I would like to find words for the many hats, dolls, curtains, cushions and lampshades that she stitched and made with such brilliance.

I think of her making something out of nothing, again and again, and of the last-minute hat she made for me to wear to a wedding.

She got a length of black tulle and knotted it at the top of my head so one end jutted out and the other back down. At the point of the knot, she stitched in garden roses with their leaves. It was a most glamorous hat and it took a matter of minutes.

And once she covered the Easter egg-shaped-card, which protects the chocolate, with soft old brown velvet, and attached a bunch of elderly black rubber grapes. I wore it to the Eastertime christening of Jazz and Lola,★ and their father took photographs of it from many angles. I keep asking if any of the photos survive, but I think not.

The car we had back then, in the late eighties, was broken into and nothing was taken except that hat; no tapes, which had been untidily rifled through, no boots or rugs or anything except the Easter egg hat, or as my mother called it, the Easter bonnet.

When I was ill as a child, she made a bonnet for Bobby the cat, who came to give me my penicillin. His ears poked through his nurse's bonnet and I smile still at the vision of the two of them. My mother had wanted to be a nurse and was always impressed by anyone who was, or who had been.

I think of all this, and mention the unpaid school fees, and burst into tears. The osteopath says: 'You have a lot of compassion for your mother,' and I can hardly bear it, I do.

I am late for the Christmas tea at the home, but I doubt if she will be at it as she finds being moved from her bed terrifying.

Maybe it's better I don't get there on time. Photographs of the summer barbecue made me sad. All the other old people look jolly, only my mother has her eyes closed and is not a part of the scene. I see a beautifully coloured-in grandfather clock with my mother's name beside it, written as if by a teacher. And think of her hands, once so strong she could twist an apple in half.

My mother never liked shows of emotion, and always found my excesses annoying, but did not want me sedated as some of her less enlightened lodgers sometimes recommended.

'I wouldn't want to break her spirit,' I once heard her telling a particularly interfering PG. My brother called him a berk and my mother wouldn't speak to my brother for a week.

'Without these people we would be out on the street,' she would say, menacingly. I was on my brother's side and remember saying to my mother: 'But he *is* a berk.'

The professor, as my mother called her dearest friend, the occupant of the room at the top, was in the kitchen when I ventured my opinion. He burst out laughing, which brought some relief because Alan possessed the wisdom we often lacked.

A Liberal candidate was at the door once, when Alan arrived and pushed past him very brusquely. The candidate asked me if he was a Tory.

I said: 'No, a mystic.'

I am among ghosts and see this time as a long day of the dead, where I am with them all before letting them rest in peace. That's my hope anyway.

My brother came back from Wisconsin, from the course in miracles, back in the nineties, and asked me if I was dead. I said: 'That is so rude, and not a question I can answer.'

DPB, as we used to call her, has sent a card to my house and I will take it along to the home, not that my mother notices them, apart from one that I signed from Bonzo.

'Ah, dear Bonzo,' she said.

DPB was a very elegant woman and, like many of my mother's friends, wealthy and bountiful. She would give my mother, her poor friend, clothes, and other unwanted items.

She once offered a carpet and my mother went round with an old pushchair, given by her friend, the road sweeper, to pull it up. Unfamiliar with the rows of tacks that lined the undersides of carpets, unseen, my mother began tugging up the carpet with her usual force. I later learned that her eight fingers were all punctured simultaneously, and blood shot out in what sounded like a cartoonish spray.

I found out about this when I noticed eight strange, chalky-looking wounds, and asked her about them.

'Oh,' she said, 'I saw some Polyfilla and stopped the blood.'

When my mother was being summarily uprooted from her home of 60 years, in the year 2003, she went into an unreachable faraway. I worked with a lawyer friend of Alan's, and with Jem, to secure her affordable housing.

The landlords were unknown offshore entities, buying up Monopoly board housing, represented by poor dupes in smart suits. One young representative called me Marcia.

'Do I get to call you Adrian?' I asked.

He was definitely attached to his position as *mister*. I said: 'You can call me Mrs Finer.'

When he said, most reasonably, that they were under no legal obligation to re-house my mother, I mentioned the ethical-moral obligation and named three well-known journalists who were very fond of my mother and would happily write the difference into national newspapers.

He asked me if I was threatening them.

'Call it what you will, Mr de Facto, I will stop at nothing.'

That defiant voice faltered, but I did stop at nothing.

In that time my mother lost the will to live, didn't take her heart pills or eat.

One day I addressed her unresponsive state.

'You know that stiff upper lip of yours I always hated? Well, I'd like to see it again now please.'

She gave me a ghost of a smile and I said, in a total role reversal: 'That's better, put a smile on your dial,' a particularly irritating thing she had often said to my sulky face.

The last night of her life in Oakley Street, she was back in a dead zone. Uriel★ had been helping me pack. His beautiful handwriting was still on some of the never-unpacked boxes I sorted through this year. He suggested we go to the cinema but I said I couldn't leave my mother.

Jem arrived and said I *must* go to the cinema, and he would help with the packing of her last things. He went into my mother's bedroom for the first time and was shocked. She never let anyone see what she called 'Steptoe's back yard'.

It was full of ladders, pots of paint, and all the tools she used to keep the rest of the house looking spotless. He threw her clothes into boxes as she had no interest in any of it. He noticed that the finger plate on her side of the door was dark and dingy. The other side was a shining example of my mother's bright brass.

The brightness she showed everyone else was not present in the little room she occupied so privately.

I guess I got to see both sides of the door, a seasonal way of seeing.

The move was good, and she had a pretty nice bedroom with no ladders or pots of paint and china-white finger plates, bright on *both* sides.

I was late for the tea party, 'with entertainer'. When I got there and said: 'I am so sorry I missed the tea,' she said: 'You missed nothing, it's so boring. Hellish in fact. So loud, and the entertainer was just wiggling like a worm with no expression.'

'Did he sing?' I asked.

'He shouted words at us and kept wiggling his bottom. He was quite good-looking, but I just wanted him to stop.'

The nurse who came with pills laughed and said: 'Your mum is usually so polite.' I amplified the gentle voice of the nurse's comment.

'I didn't say a word to him; I just closed my eyes and hoped he would go away,' said my mother.

'Very polite,' I say.

'Well, the others enjoyed it,' she said, 'I was glad to be back in my sanctum.'

'Good word,' I say.

'No, it was a ghastly party.' I laugh and change the hearing-aid batteries again.

It's good to think that after this the light will be coming back. Winter solstice is a night of hope and I am going to a bonfire to warm my pagan buns and drink *a cup o'kindness yet*, because I do like a bit of a good time, and am thrilled that so many I know now are wise and wonderful about being here.

Not everyone gets to see the spring again, but it comes anyway, and that's enough of a reason to be cheerful.

A good night for the leprechauns.

45

Here is the square-opening speech, in memory of Joe, who died this day 15 years ago:

To be called a square in English is to be dull and unadventurous. Joe was certainly no square. In fact, he was a great shape, and shape-shifter, who befriended many misfits, and I count myself proudly as one of them.

The last time I was here with Joe, in the summer of 2002, his rucksack was, as ever, full of Spanish dictionaries. Since he was a long time student of Spanish it seems only right to respect his love of this language by speaking in it. It is the language of *duende* and that particular spirit, untranslatable into English, is one which describes well the force of an extraordinary leader of lost boys and girls.

Not only in his music, but in all his actions and antics, the *duende* was apparent.

May it live on in this plaza, a square to fill with the circulation of lives that will come and go for years to come, a lasting, living space called Joe, called Joe Strummer.

I think of all the dignitaries after whom plazas have been named, and imagine all the old soldiers and authors being joined by Joe, who would no doubt find something of interest in each and every one.

Also in his rucksack of 2002 was an enormous tome on Field Marshal Montgomery of Alamein. A man as much interested in Monty's campaigns as in the poetry of Lorca was a man whose mind was never dull, a poet and a leader.

I remember seeing him lead a troupe of adventurers up a lamppost in San José, to put a pink shade on the harsh street light.

Wherever he went, Joe made the light right.

46 *NAMES*

Jem says people don't want to be named necessarily. I say: 'Oops, I've named you.'

This guarded but personal writing is causing me a bit of bother. So many people have vanished into initials, not described, just quoted.

I think of meeting a sensitive hairdresser on Hampstead Heath. Let's call him Shrew. An acclaimed author had recently written him into her latest novel, in which he's a pot-bellied, loose-lipped, dancer-shaped hairdresser.

He tells of having been quite delighted to find so many of the stories he has told, when he read the book on holiday among friends. He says that on more than one occasion he exclaimed: 'Oh, this is about you!' and read it out loud only to find further down the page that his gossipy chat had been taken down verbatim.

He had to apologise to friends. He has said more than his prayers and been robbed.

Kitty has warned me not to speak freely at Mario's, the cafe in Kelly Street. I was talking to Mario, who knows about the ageing of loved ones, and is someone with whom I feel entirely able to speak openly.

The daughter tells me that people go there to listen. She points out a case in point: One man, with a laptop and a coffee, who she says is a scriptwriter for East Enders.

I never ask her how she knows, but she says all he has to do is take down the description of my mother to get some free lines…

A few years ago, a writer called me to ask if he could interview me about my father, Imre Goth. I was taken by surprise. I asked who had given him my number. He didn't have an answer.

I said Imre was *like* a father, and then added: 'That's not quite so… He was a friend,' I tell the biographer.

I remember Imre being hounded by an insistent researcher, desperate to talk to him about Moholy-Nagy, and how Imre had made it clear that he despised the biography industry. 'Harrup harrup,' he said as if it was all just gossip.

'I'm sorry, I cannot talk to you about Imre,' I said to the voice at the other end of the line, 'but I look forward to reading the book, as there are many mysteries about my very dear friend.'

'Indeed,' the author says sincerely; and I imagine a dedicated sleuth, and am almost tempted.

I wish him well and, before hanging up, I ask what other biographies he has written. He had said, by way of introduction, that he was a published author and mentioned a recent well-received biography.

I gasped when he told me the name.

'Fanny Craddock!' I exclaim, as neutrally as I can.

Did Johnny really say, after they had been cooking doughnuts: 'May all yours turn out like Fanny's?'

'Thank you for your time, and if you change your mind, please add my number to your contacts.'

Fanny Craddock…

Names are on my mind. So many assumed names, the incognito of flight.

A few Christmases ago, I asked a rhetorical question out loud in the Horse Hospital.

'Is it name-dropping if you mention someone famous you met in a dream?'

'Yes!' shouted a bit of a genius I know.

I don't know if my dream boy is anything like the real thing, or if there is indeed a real thing. I see cosmetic looks and think of embalming before death.

In the dream we are getting on well. It is not an amorous exchange but humorous and easy.

I have noticed Jem in the corner of the dream. He has headphones on, which relieves me because otherwise I think he will be cross.

He likes the square speech, but not more talk about Joe. I don't include any more in episode 45.

It was he, Jem, and Gaby, the mother of Joe's children, who suggested I talk to the biographer way back, but I regretted how I sounded. I remember telling my mother, and she said: 'To hell with the book,' which I think the deceased would have appreciated.

My mother once gave a little speech about the brilliance of Joe. She said: 'He was a man of great intelligence and compassion. His dedication to everyone he encountered, irrespective of rank, was exemplary,' and she ended by saying: 'I consider it a great honour to have known him.'

Everyone raised their glasses: 'To Joe.'

My mother's touching words were much appreciated, especially as she has never been a great one for making speeches. In fact, it was the only one I ever heard her make. The spirit moved her.

After some time she said to me: 'Marcia, I do feel a bit embarrassed… because I thought we were raising our glasses to Jo Finer.'

Jem's uncle had also died in 2002.

'Your words were perfect for both Joes,' I reassured her.

'The young one was a delightful man,' she said, 'and always so polite.'

Today my mother said a card from my brother was 'rather Christmassy.'

I said: 'That's because it is.'

'Oh, it is, is it?' she said, in a way that made me laugh.

'It is, or at least nearly.'

I told her about last night, and the children, and she remembers Joe.

'He went too early,' she says, and I say: 'Yes' and wonder about going on time.

47

It was Christmas Eve babe, by the fish tank…

Some months ago, a high street betting shop offered a tantalising sum to adapt the Christmas song of which I never speak.

The treatment involved a WAG in a football mansion, bemoaning the Christmas fixtures. I've actually forgotten the storyline, but the unforgettable first line pops into my head and I sing it out loud.

Hush.

It's lucky the betting shop offer didn't come in last year, when I was scraping every barrel to keep my mother at home. I am relieved, this year, that the offer can be refused.

My father taught me about lies, pyramid sales, and chicanery. He railed against chain letters and shattered my belief in the promised curses. I was frightened bad luck would come my way if I were to break the chain, not only ruining my chances of getting a cascade of postcards from all over the world, but my entire life to boot.

Today I see a dreadful toy that has been so popular it has all but sold out. It is called LOL. Bare-faced cynicism is all the rage, again, this Christmas.

The appeal is in the unwrapping of it and, of course, the surprise.

You don't know what you're getting, apart from hooked. Each collectible doll has a special action, such as crying, peeing, or changing colour.

The reveal is a small plastic mutant, a big-headed saucer-eyed girl with crudely modelled yellow hair. She is wearing tiny black rubber shorts with a dummy in her mouth. She has a tattoo on her anatomically implausible thigh. The tattoo says 'Mom'.

What sort of mind has designed this monster, I wonder.

Olive tells me that there are so many of them. She wants one in a beret called Posh.

I tell her about commodity fetishism, how certain individuals make money out of selling people stories, and downright lies, attached to worthless things. I talk about cream to make you look young and ask her if she thinks it works. She doesn't.

I am my father. I remember him saying a doll I had just been given for Christmas was hideous. My sister-in-law remembers her father saying the same.

They came back from war to hate little girls' dolls, the bastards. Kitty got up early to hunt down a LOL doll.

Olive, looking at the insert, with the opportunity to collect more, asks quite casually if she can write to Father Christmas…

All you need is some pinking shears, glitter, Tippex, ribbon or string, and a hole puncher. In among so many things to do, the glitter and glue option seemed the best use of time, and, yes, later in the day I got a message from Kitty that my mother LOVES – in capitals – Olive's card, which is a last year winter scene, dabbed with glue, brushed with glitter, and spotted lightly with Tippex snow. The edges are wonky zig-zag, and the holes so close to the edge it's a miracle they hold. The shiny, thin ribbon is tied with knots so difficult to imitate that it has to be the handiwork of a serious seven-year-old.

I'm a rambler, I'm a gambler, I'm a long way from home and if you don't like me, then leave me alone I'll eat when I'm hungry, I'll drink when I'm dry, and if moonshine don't kill me, I'll live till I die…

My mother would sing this along with '*run, rabbit, run*' and '*Daisy, Daisy, give me your answer, do…*'

I never thought ill of gamblers, whether at the races or at cards, like Omar Sharif. I never thought of gambling as sad or desperate.

My mother told of a destitute cousin from England whose father had gambled away a house in Park Lane, and a country estate, in one night. His wife had died of shock.

'And did he live on?' I asked.

'Well, not for long. He'd done what he had to do,' said my mother. 'How about the daughter?' I asked.

'Well, she was a very kind woman, and held me in her arms when I woke to see my mother eating toast after my tonsils had been guillotined.'

Another horrific everyday story of my mother's.

Told she was going to a children's party, she had been confused when the maid showed her into a room with no other children, and told her to undress and get up on to a table, where a mask of gas was held to her face.

Mabel, the cousin, held my mother and sang to her gently on the way home.

Another cousin, a handsome man apparently, announced his death in *The Times* after running up debts, but then turned up and 'gave his mother a terrible fright. It nearly finished her.'

'Was he forgiven?'

'Oh yes, he was a darling, great fun,' said my mother. My mother has always had a soft spot for rogues.

She was once taken to the races and won on every horse, and said, without irony: 'If I had had the money, I'd have been a gambler.'

48 CHRISTMAS DAY, LATE

Well, it's over, and I am in my cups and not sure what to write.

It started in the morning, and on it went. The tiny top of a Harry Potter wand pen, presumed eaten by Bonzo, didn't turn up despite me poking his daily doo with a stick, to see if Dumbledore's wand tip was in the shit. No sign of it, and no sign either of the missing crew from Thunderbird 2.

I think of it as the birthday I never had. It was when I was due to be born – Christmas Day, 1957 – but I made it into the next year and am still a rooster.

Today was a long, long day in a sick bay of tinsel and fairy lights. Sammy, the two-year-old, arrived in arms, tears streaming down his face and rain pouring down behind.

It was as unlike any snowy scene of Christmas card day as could be pictured. Misery on the doorstep.

And now I can hear the poor, poorly lad crying, and wish I had a wand to make all well.

Maybe there's one in the shit.

Certainly the enthusiasm and patience of kind grown-ups is a sort of secular miracle of everyday. And this everyday day of enormous expectation is a tender pain of love.

The time I spent with my mother was calm and gentle. Bonzo looked good, a cracker hat around his neck, and the housekeeper (who is a Polish mathematician and expert bridge player), was in the room as we unpacked presents.

The home had given her a box of Dove wash and body lotion. It was a very good gift for my mother, who was always partial to Dove soap. I keep a bar, beautifully wrapped with an empty card attached, that she brought to the last Christmas dinner she spent with us, 'in case of an unexpected guest.'

She said today's boxed set was a gift from the board. She often talks about the old male residents as members of the board. I, of course, hear the pun.

Beata the housekeeper says that Christmas cactus is a misnomer, as the plant we have brought is a succulent. She talks of her mother-in-law, who was a professor of botany in Poland and died at the age of 101. She talks of bridge and how her children have no interest in the game because they suffered its importance to their parents in their childhood.

Her husband was a world champion but is now almost blind. This kind and beautiful woman lights up the lives of the old and frightened. Some days she takes Bonzo on the rounds to visit residents. He likes her very much, too.

She stays while we open presents that give some real pleasure. A hyacinth, which had already begun to sprout, was a gentle gift of new life, and a bottle of very chic *eau de parfum* gave my mother a lovely surprise.

'That's a very good one,' she says, and she's right. It smells beautiful.

Jessica's★ cheese stars were brightly packed, as were her mince pies, which she told us she had made in memory of her mother.

My mother often asks where Ann is and is repeatedly saddened to hear she has died.

Jem often says: 'Don't you think she would visit you if she were alive?' and it is, of course, quite true. Both our mothers were dutiful visitors to all in loneliness or ill-health.

When Jem and I took them on holiday to Spain, we learned a word for a pair of mothers-in-law: *las consuegras*. I remember my mother, at the other's funeral, looking like a lost child and only coming to life when Shane bent down to kiss her.

'Are you Shane?' she said, followed by, 'you were a beautiful boy.'

'I'm quite a nice old man,' he said.

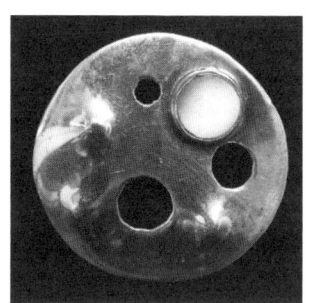

43 *Moonstone brooch made in 1989*; 44. *Bonfire*; 46. *In Bin*; 48. *My mother's spare gift*, 2013; 47. *Rocker LOL doll*; 45. *In Square*.

'Go on with you,' she said, and looked quite cheered.

She always said how beautiful he was, and that he was a country boy.

Today she was sad to hear of Ella's ill-health, and that of little Sammy, and said she wished she could get out of her bed and help. I said I wished she could, too.

It was good to see her, and the glitter from Olive's card on her face was a sign that she had been looking at the little girl's gift. It was hanging by her bed with the snow scene to the wall and the bright little school portrait facing her.

This time is easier for her than last year, and she reports quite cheerily on the frequent visits from the baby elephant that sits in the corner and sometimes pees on the chair.

Jem wonders what it means. I think the elephant in the room is *death,* but this baby is quite a cheery presence and my mother says the little elephant has a lovely expression.

There are so many Christmases in my mind as I tune out of this one, tapping towards the morning and glad we all found reasons to be cheerful in the bleak midwinter.

49

I catch the minder rolling his or her eyes; an androgynous figure is instructing me on how to get away with a crime. He or she shares disbelief with the driver of the taxi, who is a middle-aged *lovely* with a big fluffy mane of hair. She drives away, and then I am ripped from this dream by intense cramp in both calves. I groan as the muscles clench in excruciating pain.

I can't remember the details of the crime or the flight, only that it was such a great yarn. I remember thinking this dream could have been written by John Buchan, and I remember an acid yellow and black clutch purse. A handbag by any other name, or vagina of course.

I fall asleep again, trying to remember the case of Dora, Herr K, and Frau K. And wonder if there are any clues in Freud as to how I can go about anonymising.

I think of how Freud used the name Dora as an alias in his analysis of a case of hysteria. Dora was the name of a maid in the Freud household who also had had to be renamed. She could not be called Rosa, her given name, because his sister was already called Rosa. I love the name Dora. I hear 'door' and 'adore'.

I fell asleep on the dream purse and woke thinking of the late Christmas post and Giles.

That name came about on a bus from Dublin airport, when Jem said something about where we were to meet Shane and I said '*Ssshhh…* call him something else. He's a household name here.' 'Giles,' said Jem, and it stuck.

Giles's birthday gig is coming after I myself will have finished pushing 60, and so I won't be tempted to name names.

It's not easy living in a society so split between sycophants and begrudgers, who are so often, as Giles himself once pointed out, the self-same persons.

He responded lovingly to a long-gone deep distress I experienced over being pushed out of the company of my old friends by the new proprietors, members of the board or whoever.

All those who do not suck it up or play by the rules of the new order are dumped, jettisoned, traded in, and that is how the crooked cookie crumbles.

There is such a big collusion at the stinking heart of fame and fortune.

It's not like the storybooks, where the sensitive runt sets off on a life journey and listens to the advice of animals and misshapen beings. That runt is open to the ugly and the unfamiliar, and does not rely on the polished knobs of accredited position. In this way the runt survives and gets the crown, which is, of course, all about being your own sovereign self.

The handsome big brothers have no ear for the misshapen, the crones or animals, no time for the ugly, and so they must perish.

I understood this from Bruno Bettleheim's thesis on the uses of enchantment. I learned a lot from his writing and was devastated to hear of his cruelty to the children in his care.

'You can be sure of nothing,' as my mother was wont to say, and to which I said, and still say, '*Yay oh yay.*'

'He belongs to all of us now,' said an Oxbridge-educated filmmaker, as he pushed me out of the way to get to Jem after a gig on a boat. I'd just had a baby and was still sore because my life as an equal was threatened. Big brothers do not perish outside of fairy tales. *Alas.*

I think of obsequious courtiers, and, how in the hour of my howling grief, back in the mid-eighties, Giles said he had been bothered about the be-grudgers and wanted to prove he wasn't the idiot they said he was. And then, of course, with fame came the same crowd recast into a needy lot of self-important sycophants.

He told me not to bother with them, and that I was lucky and should look at who thought I was great.

'Who?' said I.

'Jem and me,' he said, without bothering to swell the ranks.

50 SCHISM, JISM, ETC.

The last big 0 I had was full of people I don't know anymore. It's been a decade of changes and I'm not the only one.

SR had a dream in which a man's voice to one side called 'all change', and I thought she dreamed for me too. Actually, I think the dream applies to us all. But being well trained not to speak on behalf of others, and fearful of being taken for a cult leader, I will speak only for myself.

I think of Jung, and big fights and fallings out between once deeply-resonating minds.

The 'ego orgasm', as a creepy psychiatrist lady once called the thrill between myself and a now-vanished best friend.

Like and unlike minds.

'You give each other ego orgasms,' she said. I think she wanted to have them with him as she seemed to like it when we fell out.

Only complain of trouble with another to someone who likes that other, or you just give glee to the listener. I used to tell my children that, and I always do it myself.

He gave her glee by telling her of my irreligiosity.

Luckily I know a kind and intelligent psychiatrist, or I would veer towards contempt for the whole lot of them. I can still hear, 'Physician, heal thyself,' bursting from my rude voice box when I occasionally have to listen to their pontifications.

So, who put the pontiff in their Hippocratic oath?

We fell from grace with each other because I would not bring up my daughters in the faith.

A recent convert to Catholicism via pleasuring priests, he stood up and let a seven-year-old girl fall to the floor. He had been filling her head with a dream of the little white bridal outfit of First Communion.

He easily won a convert and said to the child on his knee: 'Ask your mother.'

I burst into tears and gave an impassioned speech as to why such children should never be indoctrinated like that.

'Did you know a requiem mass was sung for Hitler in Dublin? Have you no respect for their Jewish blood? Do you not realise why I would never want our daughters to have to subscribe to a belief system that forbids abortion, a creed that denies homosexuality?!'

At that I spat, he stood up, the child fell to the floor and the proselytiser left.

After the departure I sobbed, choking on all the blind eyes turned on abuse. I had not only seen, but been under such eyes.

I loved Jesus and Bobby the cat best of all as a small child, and I can still see why. The animal, and the kindest of humans, appeal to me still. I'm always hoping Jesus will come back, as I think some of his supporters would get a nasty and necessary shock.

I have accepted the invitation to be a godmother and think of Efua's wonderful naming ceremony in Brixton when, like a pale-faced colonial at a ceremony of otherness, I looked aghast as a bottle of fine spirit was thrown on the carpet.

The elder conducting the service stopped and explained to me that libations were being offered to the ancestors. I love this idea.

My other experience was in Edinburgh, when the cardinal I later called Sin conducted the rituals of First Communion. I was standing by the godfather, an elderly character actor, himself a character of great wit and charm.

'Look at our one,' he said in the hushed tones of a stage whisper, 'the only one taking it seriously.'

It was true. All the other little girls and boys in white were loving the attention of the big day. Only our one had his eyes fixed on far-off mystery and devotion.

In George Harrison's mansion, imagining what goings on went on in the sumptuous bathroom, I became another sort of godparent.

Downstairs, a poster warned that pizza, fast cars and girls in mini-skirts only lead the wrong way.

The little boy, on his first day of rice, gazed out like a tiny deity and gave deep, unusual eye contact to each and every one of us. That day I said: 'If this baby was a religious leader, I'd sign up.'

My sister says something about the cathedral nativity scene including more 'dusky skin tones' and how this pleases her, as the blonde, blue-eyed figures had always seemed wrong.

We agree that the down-to-earth shepherds and the starry royalty, the Magi, make a good social mix along with the creatures, and we talk about refugees and flight from places called home.

I have recently been having such similar thoughts so I feel a deep connection with my older sister, who had become a relative stranger down the years.

She remembers taking me on a holiday with her then-boyfriend in Ireland, and how they laughed when I kissed the Blarney Stone. She had been nursing the father of my mother's best friend Biddy, and the bachelor son of advanced years became enamoured of his father's nurse.

He was a little boy at Miss Aherne's school and my mother remembers him hopping everywhere.

I tried to make myself scarce and took a long bus ride into Dublin most days to look at the Book of Kells. The pages were turned every day back then. The elderly father was worried I never ate but then, neither did he.

I liked him a lot and wish I could have stayed, smoking and drinking with him, but the lovers took me on a trip to Kinsale and my sister spoke sternly at the outset:

'Do *not* say you are a descendant of Oliver Cromwell.'

I hadn't been planning to give out such information, but my sister feared I said such things to get a reaction.

At one point she thought I had purposefully drawn a vulva in a game where drawing was a key component. I said: 'It's an eye, and I wouldn't even know what a vulva looks like.'

Looking back, I see her patience, although the drawing caused a row as she thought I was being a smart arse and teasing the Irish bachelors, but I really wasn't. I only wish I had been. The call was good, and so was the walk yesterday, with good friends and perfect strangers.

I am happy that my Oyster for the over sixties has been approved, and am already looking forward to free travel.

My mother enjoyed marzipan today and I noticed a box of chocolates from Cincinnati. 'Has MH been to visit?'

'Oh yes,' says my mother, who looks rather pleased.

She says: 'He is not getting old,' when I say Jem is getting a cold. She finds this very funny when I amplify the misunderstanding, and laughs.

After leaving my mother, I met a poet that I hadn't seen for twenty years. He asked me when we had last met.

I said: 'I'm not the person to ask anymore. I might have known once, but now I really don't.'

I continued the conversation by asking: 'When do you live?'

'Oh,' I said, 'I meant *where* but I kind of prefer *when*.'

He said he much preferred *when,* followed by 'Stoke Newington.'

'The amount of energy that I put in was fucking mental, Casey,' says a loud, irate voice outside my window.

The other one says: 'You are quite something,' and the conversation moves on up the street and out of earshot.

I take note. Time to stop.

51

Am sitting in an African night very aware of what children we are, most fraught in the web of memories, almost inventions.

Wrote that last night and couldn't go further… And then he did.

I woke to a beautiful message from my brother about my upcoming birthday, and it almost seemed like the cod pieces of our lives were finding a resting place, understanding nothing but love, a better option to all the other expressions of difference and dismay.

Wondering on in this time of pushing 60…

I wasn't so well today and was going about my business lost in thoughts, with at least one rude awakening.

My darling 4-year-old grandson jumped on my head in a burst of enthusiasm, but the shock and pain had me howling. Ever since I fell off the side of a ditch in the summer, my neck has been a mess.

When Jem first saw me staring at him, from a row of TEFL beginners, he wondered how such a tiny neck could support such a big head. It *is* a miracle.

Today I screamed out loud and terrified the poor little boy who could not say sorry.

'It is very difficult,' he explained with utmost sincerity when pushed into the impossible word by his mother and grandfather.

I suggested he might prefer to say 'lorry', and I would know what it meant. After kicking his mother and hitting his grandfather, the poor child had two more impossible sorries to add to his list.

In the most pathetic scene, he said sorry three times.

Love is never having to say you're sorry, was a poster slogan which caused me great,

great mirth. I once tried it on my mother, back in the very early seventies, and it didn't go down well.

I think of another little boy, forced to say sorry, who raged at his mother that she had told him never to lie, but then had *forced* him to lie as he was not sorry.

Smart kid. Lucky for you to have adults that understand your righteous indignation and see the funny side.

And I remember my brother once saying if our father had only said he was sorry that he had fucked it all up, then he wouldn't have had to go mad.

I am sorry. Sorry to say…

No, I'm not sorry I'm sorry; I *am* sorry. So sorry, I'm not sorry.

The best sorry I ever said was not accepted. I was so magnanimous to be the first to say sorry, and it was rejected. Then I knew I wasn't sorry at all.

52 *BLOODSTREAM*

I am not sure that turning anything inner into outer is worthwhile today. Maybe it's a day of quiet. Remembering aloud is not a habit I wish to cultivate. It's an experiment to see if going backwards and forwards in a daily piece of writing is even doable.

My brother and sister are on my mind, as the relative strangers of my whole life.

They came so long before me that my mother calls them her 'children', her 'family', and when I ask, she says that I am her 'friend'.

This pleases me, but I am not quite over the sadness of coming from the same blood and feeling so estranged.

My mother used to say, 'built in the same shipyard' jauntily, to anyone who remarked on the similarity of our looks. She laughed at those who recoiled from the comment.

Shipyards and shipbuilding seem as far away as the Titanic. Harland and Wolff, just names.

My mother sometimes tells of a baby she saved from the Titanic, and which she holds close because she has been told to look after it. She holds it close to her for years, but finally must return it, so she takes it to a big house where the baby is welcomed and my mother is thanked for her help.

My friends who hear this say they think the baby is me, but I don't see why, and they never can say.

I know my mother always thought dreaming of a baby meant death. I compare her strange lexicon of dream symbols with Freudian ones. I have never asked what dreaming of a handbag means to her.

Long ago, I dreamed of being handed a baby that wriggled and squirmed so perilously in my arms that I ran into a vast empty space in a long-ago New York.

I knew this place from movies. It was a vacant lot, surrounded by high wire fences. I saw a lone figure standing in the centre. I wanted to give the baby away. I ran to the man and saw it was Joe. I thrust the baby into his arms, which he placed around the baby, who became easy and calm.

I was going to leave it, but he said: 'Hey, it's yours,' and so I prepared my arms in imitation of his.

Once rigid and ready, I said: 'Okay, give it back.'

As he placed the baby in my dead-set embrace, he said: 'It will move, and then you will have to move.'

I was so struck by the good advice that it woke me.

In analysis at the time I was asked about the baby, and I said it was creativity. I didn't mumble out the word as if it was contaminated with wrongness, as I sometimes found myself doing at that time. I said it out loud and clear. Later when I told Joe the dream, he said it was a good dream for him, too.

It was around this time that I went back to the Slade as a mature student, and I felt so old at 33 and frightened of dropping that particular baby again.

I dreamed of another baby, at this now long-gone time of starting over. A female infant with an apple-green face, black body and limbs. She was the most beautiful human I had ever seen, and I disagreed with the great Germaine Greer, who I have only met in this one dream. She was sure the baby was wrong, and I told her: 'I am sorry, *you* are wrong; this baby is *perfect*.'

It is curious to be so far away from the humans who can remember you coming into being. My brother and sister, so the story goes, were squabbling the night I was born, and my father put a laundry basket between them.

They must have been sharing a bed. I never thought of that before.

I know they knew about the plan to give me away, but they cannot say anything about it.

If I was being carried by a mother who thought she would have to part from the unseen life within her, I can only imagine panic – in the amniotic fluids.

I imagine carrying loss for all those months, under tidy and pleasantly co-ordinated maternity smocks and slacks.

I was touched by my sister approving of the new figures in the Cathedral's nativity scene. 'More dusky tones,' as she put it. I appreciate the slightly old-fashioned language.

I remember my sister as a student nurse, and how I would wave *Fair Pay for Nurses* streamers out of our dead father's Mini Traveller, which she had inherited, and drove fast, while dragging on Bensons with me screaming out of the window.

She used to go to events to raise consciousness and funds to free Zimbabwe, and was sometimes the only white girl at the party.

53 *SPIRALS*

You will not get what you want, don't worry!

I find this curious message, written messily on masking tape, stuck into a page of notes I made about the Isle of Man as a wartime detention centre.

And I go down a big hole called '53' and smell again the black linoleum of the horrible house polished by a maid called Esperanza.

Polished by hope, and never happy.

I think of Pissy Farquhar, arriving looking for Bohemia, bored by Brown's and of being told of brothels on O Street.

I see the beautiful little dark haired girl, opening the door to the tall man in uniform, and finding out from her sister that there was a vacant room for the officer.

He asked her to run him a bath, and the geyser★ blew itself off the wall. (If not an omen, then what?) My mother ran down to the actress in the basement and asked if a pilot could have a bath in her bathroom.

The actress was, of course, only too pleased to help the war effort, and so my mother turned on the taps for the second time and went to tell the officer the good news.

He said: 'Thank you,' and that was all.

She went to her sister and said: 'Charm is not his middle name.' His middle name was in fact Churchill, which pleased my grandmother.

Where he thought he was finding the real McCoys, he was not, but that is quite another story.

There are many 'quite other' stories, and some which I find so brilliant as they fade. Who was the lodger who asked my mother, when the war was over, if she had never wondered why he had left once a month without word? It was something to do with full moon and hush-hush work, but what was the silent business on the moonlit sea between Harwich and the hook of Holland?

Maybe my mother will remember tomorrow, as she has asked me if Denny Vaughan is still playing. Denny had wanted to be a pilot, but was such a gifted musician and singer that the Canadian authorities ordered him to sing through the war.

'He was as good as Sinatra,' remembers my mother, dreamily, and I wonder if she ran him a bath.

I did once know the name of the actress, and the spy, but it's all going, going, almost gone.

Today she says she has been stitched-up and has had to endure a general anaesthetic and extreme discomfort to rectify the mistake.

What happened, as I went down into the number by which home was known, was that a ping brought me back from '53' and alerted me to a wonderful moment of encouragement. Tanya had just called my work *worthwhile* and I thrilled to the unusual word of praise.

Her Eminence, Tanya Peixoto, the current Vice-Curatrice of the Collège de Pataphysique, no less. Elected in 2014 to succeed Her Magnificence Lutembi, a crocodile.

I am very proud of being awarded a Grand Gidouille, a big spiral. I will never forget being given the best certificate of my life.

I was attending a formal night of honours – or would they be *dishonours?* – in Paris at the College and had not been expecting any pataphysical attention, otherwise, as I said in my acceptance speech, I would have had my hair done and remained sober.

I was presented with the certificate by none other than the great and minute Fernando Arrabal, wearing one pair of spectacles above the other.

Gavin Bryars had just become a Satrap that night, a most notable member anyway, and I was already delighted. At the call to the stage I burst with delight.

I like the men who are notable members: Marcel Duchamp; Man Ray; Groucho, Chico *and* Harpo Marx; Max Ernst and Joan Miró to name but some.

I am so happy to hear my writing has been deemed *worthwhile* by the siren of all imaginary solutions.

54

Couldn't sleep this New Year's Eve dawn and, advised not to read breaking news, I go for opinion and personal problems.

Hours passed in reading advice to an unhappy family member, ranging from, 'leave at once, don't turn back,' to 'have you no heart, these are the people who gave you life and cared as best they could.'

An article on Helen Garner and her recognition, at 75, for years and years of ingenious compulsive work, a salve for the spitefulness she says she has felt over the missing accolades and awards came with the dawn birds.

And then to the so-called New Year's Honours list.

Clegg might be just the nicest chap to play ping pong with, or accompany on a visit to the Alhambra, but it is a crying shame he got into the Cameron government. Is this knighthood a booby prize? A big, blue, booby handle?

Jeremy Hillary Boob PhD is the nowhere man, living in the sea of nothing (back to nothing again) in the yellow submarine, of course. This dentist/botanist/artist/writer/physicist/nobody was voiced by Dick Emery.

Dick Emery, *ooh, you are awful, but I like you.*

Ringo Starr invited the Boob along, who turned out to mend the submarine and be a great help against the forces of evil.

And from Jeremy Boob to Ringo and another K, as they say.

I always loved Ringo Starr when I was a kid. John loved John and I loved Ringo. George was so beautiful, I put his picture up later when they came for free in *The White Album*, which my sister had but didn't want the pictures.

No boys liked George, if I remember. They especially didn't seem to like *While My Guitar Gently Weeps*. They never wanted to play that on their guitars. Hum *My Sweet*

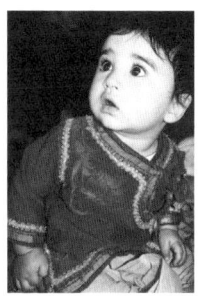

49. *Giles and Jem and Marcia* (1984); 50. *Oshin*; 51. *Love Story*, 1970; 53. *La Grande Gidouille*, 2015; 54. Boob; 52. *The S.S. Titanic*.

Lord at a boy and you could dispel the keenest interest.

Something is another matter. *I don't know, I don't know…*

I remember my 16th birthday and the great crystal rock round Johnny Eagle's neck, given to him by a master at Westminster. Or so he said.

I got him to sign the Jimi Hendrix record he had brought. 'Thanks for seeing me thru the bad times, sincerely Johnny Eagle.' He wrote 'thru' spelled with 4 letters.

I loved him, and thought he looked a bit like Paul McCartney.

He went out with the older sister of my friend, so I had plenty of time to admire this quite-plump boy who wore blue suede shoes, a big crystal, and who wrote a rock opera called *Harold* with my friend Julian.

I played Ringo Starr's solo album at that party. Sir Ringo. I don't think the guests found it cool but I thought: '*You come on like a dream, peaches and cream, you're sixteen, you're beautiful, and you're mine,*' was written for me and I danced to it alone, singing to myself in a no-boy-no-girl dance.

I am asked what I am doing for my 60th. Maybe something like that.

It's New Year's Eve and it's all over, the mayor's fireworks have lit up the distant Eye, which vibrated in anticipation of the big midnight that comes like any other, but with knobs on.

I remember one New Year's Eve when I was eleven my mother was very enthused by the poem about a man who stood at the gate of the year.

The next New Year's Eve she pulled down the one-year-old, grease-splattered card and said: 'Well that was a bloody awful one, to hell with the man who stands at the gate of the year.'

Oh, we larfed.

California is decriminalising weed today, and I am with my very dear friend from Hamburg, who has brought me a drawing of myself as a charm-school era lovely in a saucy shepherdess outfit. It says: 'Painted from memory.'

The little hand holds a cigarette, as now. It's the New Year and I still haven't stopped. And I know they do what it says on the packet.

And curse Sir Walter Raleigh; he was such a stupid get. I always heard *get,* not *git.*

Oh well, here we go, into another day. Too, late as it's already here and, according to my esoteric friends, a challenging year with many bust-ups and revelations to come. I think that is a safe bet by way of a prognosis.

But, for what it's worth, I do wish 'Happy New Years' and, like any old numbskull, wish for peace and love.

'If you say it out loud, your wish doesn't come true,' say the seriously wishful. Well, I sure hope they're wrong and I haven't jinxed the peace and love wish. Happy New Year.

55

'He would have taken you to the top and made sure everyone knew who had escorted you there.'

I say this of a predator who used rank to seduce beautiful young men with dreams of fame. Rank is a good word for it. The rank organisation.

My friend from Hamburg went to sleep as I read out my Forever Eve episode and says, this morning: 'It felt safe.'

He tells me the German greeting for this time can be translated as: 'Slip well into the New Year.' I hear: '*Sleep well* into the New Year.'

I fell asleep on the tube, answering a New Year's Day message from my brother saying something about our father, that after 50 years there is a thaw. He doesn't put it into such fridge-freezer language, but says:

'For all this time I have carried him frozen in my heart as an incurable wounding.' And then goes on to write something about that which has begun to melt.

'More than that I can say, but must admit that writing it down is a stumbling affair.'

I love that, and understand the stumbling affair. It is a good message, as I have felt a bit deep in the freeze of it all myself.

And I like how he ends: 'Let the sorrow be love.' And why not?

I think of suffering being so over-privileged once, and how it wasn't just gay men who responded to all those wounds, it was me too.

When we got to find out suffering and redemption were for sissies, I kept clandestine faith in it.

'Suffering has transformational potential,' I sometimes said out loud, and was poo-pooed by the sophisticated.

My mother looks at me and says: 'You poor little girl, you look exhausted,' and I say: 'I am a bit.'

Paulo stops the supper trolley in the corridor and says the tickets for the fireworks were fifty pounds, and we agree that it is a shocking price for ten minutes. He says in Italy they are bigger, better, last longer, and are free.

I say: 'This is England.' My mother says: 'Is it?'

And I laugh, which makes her laugh.

William, the resident who says: 'Don't make me laugh,' to nearly everything I say, comes out of his room and smiles at me, and this makes me very happy as I have been on a mission to report a missing Christmas gift, the good *eau de parfum*, and I feel the prickly sadness of an elderly child failing to make all well.

56 HYPNOSIS

I hear from an auld lang syne.

Yesterday, New Year's Day, I heard from a friend in Berlin with the name of a hypnotherapist. I had asked for the name and address so long ago I had quite forgotten the interest I had once shown.

Hypnosis sticks in my head as an entertainment I have never appreciated. I see perfectly sensible members of the dinner-and-show audience clucking like chickens, pushing out their backsides to lay big, imaginary eggs.

I wonder if such vaudeville was once a shadowy staple of black and white TV, along with *Steptoe and Son*.

I showed such interest because my friend had been delivered from the pain and fear of primal abandonment in one long, sobbing day.

I phone the number and mention smoking. He's expensive, but cheaper than cigarettes.

After calling, I choke on a baked potato skin. I bang on the table, which I remember is the international non-verbal SOS for such a situation.

But nobody knows this, and so the life-saving thump is a long time coming. I have always loved potato skins.

When Mama Cass inhaled a ham sandwich, one of my school friends asked me, under her breath: 'What is a ham sandwich?'

I explained that it was a ham sandwich. She had suffered the shame of not knowing what 'cold turkey' was. But she wasn't the only one.

I said I was really interested in anger, much to her older brother's surprise when he mentioned he was going to see some Anger films at the Electric. He said something about *Scorpio Rising*.

'Anger is a filmmaker,' she explained again so as not to be heard, 'his favourite.'

I covered my innocence and bluffed my way through an interest I had never had.

But later, watching Nazi boys in an occult silent movie with great music, which must have been *Lucifer Rising*, I felt quite at home in the odd excess, and loved the sight of smoke in the beam from the projector. Cinema isn't nearly as sexy these days.

Oops, none of that. Smoke is not attractive.

Apparently, Cass Elliot died in her sleep of a heart attack. A ham sandwich was on her bedside table, not blocking her windpipe, but how would I know, I wasn't there.

I look up hypnosis. Good for weight control, alcoholism, substance abuse, grief, loss and, of course, anger.

If it works, then why are there so many fat, angry, lonely, sad, substance-abusing losers?

Without wishing to romance greedy people, I am at home in slight excess, and am having to kick myself to remember the doctor's orders to drink moderately.

Last year I met a South American mystic called Marcia, and it was odder even than I can remember. She had the gift of speaking along with any language, accompanying, rather than anticipating whatever was said, in any tongue.

She told me to give up alcohol and I wasn't even drinking when she gave this advice, but I had just been thinking how much I'd like a glass of wine. I hadn't said a word out loud. It was all most peculiar and seems like a dream to me now, but there were witnesses, and sometimes her calling card appears among my papers and notes.

I consider my trip to Finchley, to see the hypnotherapist tomorrow, as a cornily good fit in terms of the looking-back-so-as-to-look-forward thrust of *Pushing 60*.

I think again of John, known as Johnny, who died at the age of 56, two years after a herring saved his life. He never pushed 60, my ancient old father with a cravat over the hole in his neck.

It did cross my mind that choking on a potato skin would have given the whole *Pushing 60* project quite a stunningly unexpected end.

Killingly funny.

But I am still here, tapping on. And thinking on the number numbly.

I reflect on another communication from the Vice-Curatrice, who writes:

'When you reach 60, could you perhaps (please) extend it to *Pushing 63*? After all that is the age Dr Faustroll was when he was born.'

I ponder this as I fall asleep on my lap.

The unique life of Dr Faustroll is indeed a wonder: born and dead in the same extraordinary year for pataphysics, 1898.

This is now 120 years ago, and 60 years is half that time ago. I was born a mere 60 years after Dr Faustroll.

57 *RELAX*

'Where are you?'

'Nowhere.'

'Who is with you?'

'Nobody.'

'What are you feeling?'

'Nothing.'

I cannot lie.

My thigh is cold and there is a mouldy smell that keeps me from going deeper.

'Relax, and just let yourself…'

Oh dear, all that money and I can't even damn well relax. It's the word *relax* that triggers panic.

I didn't mind Frankie saying relax. I loved it, in fact.

Relax, don't do it, when you wanna go to it Relax, don't do it, when you wanna come!

Or when you want to go into, or out of, your mind.

My brother sends a message from our father, who communicated something to him last night:

'Live into your dying.'

I have considered this today and wonder if it is actually what I am trying to do.

When my mother asks after my brother, I say that John Farquhar, our father, has been in touch with him.

I have presumed she would be fine with this, given her ease with visitors from other dimensions and their communications.

'Is he back in the loony bin?' she asks.

Our friend from Hamburg is in the room, and laughs at the unexpected voice of reason from the pillow.

My mother is very pleased to see him and says she has always loved him and remembers her trip to Germany to stay with him. She explains she had never wanted to go to Germany on account of Fraulein Gertrude Schuffner.

She spits out the name, and he laughs and says, 'You were not so fond of her.'

My mother talks of how the steward's wife told the steward, who told her father…

The story drifts through so many members of staff, till we get to the bleeding knuckles. For every wrong note played on the piano, the governess would slash her across the back of her hands with a ruler. She pulled her by the hair to get her home quickly.

'Fraulein was in a hurry to complete her duties so she could race off to meet the postman, with whom she was having a passionate love affair.'

My mother always adds 'love' to 'affair' just as some add 'train' to 'station.' Love jars in this hateful tale.

There is no mention of the postman tonight, nor the SS officer she went home to marry, nor the time she left Sunday lunch to get a handkerchief when my mother's father had said: 'Fraulein, tell us all about this Mr Hitler of yours,' in what must have sounded a disrespectful tone.

My mother adds: 'She was a very cruel woman, and German of course.'

'We are not all so cruel,' says Herr Noll, and the carer, who has been sitting with a spoon of pea soup suspended for minutes, laughs at this but adds kindly: 'Nobody's gonna hit your fingers for a wrong note girl.'

And I feel love for this beautiful woman and man.

My mother is still sure she has been stitched up and has had to endure hours of surgery to rectify the situation. She explains the awful details of the mistaken procedure and speaks openly of orifices while she holds hands with the good German.

The carer says that my mother has told her that her son is dead.

I mention this casually, and my mother, looking unfazed, tells me that when she rang the hospital they said they thought he had died in the night, 'but it was just some little girl answering the phone who had got her lines crossed.'

58

My mother remembers something I once said and laughs. 'If there's one thing I hates, it's walking and weeding.' I did say that. I remember it's all we seemed to do.

I love walking, but weeding not so much, mainly because of fox shit. I hate foxes staring at me in the little back garden.

I blame Jem, and other nature lovers, for the fearless foxes of North London. Some people leave food out for them so they don't get mange.

Mange, manger, away in a manger…

Some are fat now, and look back with what Werner Herzog once called: 'the cold hard stare of nature.'

Bonzo barks at them, but they aren't bothered by the poodle, unless I lift him up and together we become a super-sized, barking, shouting, creature of outrage. B. Trotwood and dog.

Last night I got the most wonderful message, late, when I was not falling asleep. It was from Stephen Hodge, who I met on a bus in a heat-wave.

I was pushing a heavy trolley, modelled on a RyanAir one, up and down the tight aisle, selling flocked twigs, paintings by me, and old nighties. I was giving away warm fizzy drinks, Twiglets, and Pringles with which to make duck lips.

I think Stephen was the only person who bought anything.

He bought a green flocked twig by Peggy Atherton,★ my brilliant friend who cast roadkill way back in the nineties.

Cadbury's once gave unlimited free chocolate to art student casters. She made *Easter Bunny*, which was a road-kill hare with visible tyre mark, or so I remember, it got into the papers and caused a stink.

The suppliers had never stipulated what was to be made, or not made, but wanted to disown the chocolate road-kill.

Ahead of her time, she was into flocking long before useless gift shops made flocked anything/everything. Her twigs and branches, like antlers, were as curious and marvellous as her tiny cast-porcelain insects.

Peggy was the sculptor who helped me cast my rosebud, and one of the best soundtracks to my entire life is the bafflement we shared looking at the negative spaces in the alginate.

'That's it. No, that's it.'

Stephen Hodge was known to me as a part of the Situationist group Wrights and Sites, and their ingenious mis-guides, but I first met him on that hot bus.

I don't see or hear from him often, so was very pleased to receive a message last night. It was such a lovely one, and so poignant, and this sentence impressed and moved me deeply:

'Oddly, my flamboyant cousin Marion, Somerset County Council's first woman rat-catcher, made me think of you today as she conjured up family stories at my mother's wake.'

I think of mothers, going and gone, and the living, who relieve our sadness.

I love the sound of Somerset County Council's first woman ratcatcher being the family storyteller at the wake.

59 *PENULTIMATE*

Tying up and unfolding.

It's almost over and out, this preamble.

Mouse droppings followed the cheese I took home and lost down the radiator. Cause and effect.

Bonzo killed a mouse but didn't tease it, like cats so often do. 'There is no love of life without despair of life.' Camus said that.

I have just had another cigarette and am contemplating the appointment with the hypnotherapist, whose voice doesn't send or soothe me. I have downloaded the voice telling me to relax, and I don't like it.

I love John Cale's voice, and can imagine burrowing down into the far-out depths of the unknown, with warm thighs, hearing his hypnotic guidance.

The osteopath understands, and wonders if so much correction is a good thing. Me too. I wonder, too.

I loved the ballad of Waldo Jeffers and used to listen again and again. My brother said John Cale sounded like our father, who was not Welsh but had a similarly beautiful blankness and resonance.

MH has a similar pitch, so now I wonder if my mother also responds to the low unexcitable voices of intelligent men.

It became obvious that the mention of Mark, the first name of both MH and Herr Noll, threw my mother.

I now see why she didn't accept the German visitor, at first, as being the expected Mark.

She says she has a passion for him. For whom? Who is he? I think Éamon de Valera and MH have morphed together.

I am slightly concerned that this is confidential and I shouldn't be spilling beans.

I am out of town now, and almost asleep. It's the beginning of the birthday proceedings.

On the dinner table is a little telly screen showing sleeping children. We are in a child and pet-friendly hotel.

Unexpectedly, the spying device vibrates, blinks, howls and turns into a call for action.

There is human back-up, a kind boy comes to say Bonzo has been wailing. Creatures are in need of comfort. Joe and Jem go to offer the only thing worth a fuck, kindness.

Jem's father, Sammy, looked like Picasso and was often mistaken for him. He once had his photo taken, alongside his own brilliant brothers, with the Marx brothers in Paris. The Jewish brothers in a photograph that can only be imagined, as nobody can find it.

This morning I put lipstick on in front of a mirror and saw, in the reflection, my mother, in a portrait by Imre, and Sammy smiling out from the backside of one of his books.

In my cups and falling asleep on the keys, I am pleased to think of having shared time on the planet with such fabulously fictional real people.

I laugh to myself and think back to Herr Noll's visit.

My mother asks about his wife.

I say: 'He is not the marrying kind,' which, for any younger listeners, is an old euphemism. My mother looks relieved.

I have booked up to go to Dublin for quite a few days, to walk the streets looking for my mother. I imagine having pushed 60 with a living mother.

Of course, there is still time for that not to be the case.

From nine years old onwards, I dreaded the feared death of the other much-loved ambivalent parent, and planned ahead for my position as full orphan.

Not so long ago my mother said to Katy that: 'Marcia always said she was going to live with your mother if anything happened to me.'

Katy found it touching and pragmatic that I had made such a choice so early on. Speaking too soon is a habit of mine.

'Isn't this the most unexpectedly happy day,' I might announce, just before it goes terribly wrong.

This is the penultimate.

I might die between now and then. 'Then' being tomorrow.

60

It's only a few hours since my last episode and it's on my mind, it's woken me.

No, this is my last; that was my *latest*.

This is the ultimate, however shit, and it's Epiphany.

I wrote those lines before sunrise, and now it is after sunset.

There is doubt, no neat plot. Nothing has happened, and so much of it.

60 years so far.

I'm here. I'm alive. Me too.

Not quite On Kawara, but not entirely unlike.

This goes out on Twitter, a few people press *like* or *retweet*. I notice and am very pleased. You know who you are, and I thank you.

Older schoolchildren, I read, are in danger of being overwhelmed by the need to be liked on social media.

I can understand this. People can be mean.

My mother said I lived on her nerves, which is mean, but also clever.

I will take flowers tomorrow and thank my mother for having me, and keeping me, and being an inspiration. Truly.

And now to end on ancient rocks and mysterious time and what nobody knows, which is always most relieving.

Looking up the standing stones at Avebury, I come across the name Ross Nichol. I remember that bulbous-nosed old warlock on Parliament Hill, back in 1968 when I was a young assistant to spring.

Ross Nichol was a friend of Olivia's, the High Priestess of Isis. He interpreted the significance of Avebury for a new generation of druids.

55. *Fireworks*; 58. Peggy Atherton, *Easter Bunny*, 2000; 56. Kenneth Anger, *Rabbit's Moon*; 60. *Sheep at Avebury;* 59. *Old Friends;* 57. *Wires.*

Through him, I encounter a very agreeable new leader★ of druids today. He speaks of pitching in and getting on with it, not letting fear of failure stop us living.

He suggests ditching *real* and *unreal* as oppositional; if you have an experience that is soothing or uplifting, not to worry if it is real or unreal.

'Fire the filing clerk,' he says.

I think this is timely advice.

He talks of inner growth connected to the outer plant world, and about protecting that world. I love all this and think of weeding.

The stones of Avebury cause me a wonderful deep silence and awe. It is a good place to come any day, but on Epiphany it is too cosmic for words.

The Magi really brought on the mystery for me, following a star as they did.

I love that the day of the kings is celebrated in Spain and it is they, the greatest gift givers ever, that bring the sweets and the toys, not old FC, with flying reindeer and sack of crap.

Spanish children leave water for the camels.

ENDNOTES

Page 13. Sandra Bartoli is the co-founder of the architecture office Büro für Konstruktivismus in Berlin and co-publisher of the architectural journal *Architektur in Gebrauch (AG)*. 'Her architecture is always about telling stories – often like a garden of forking paths, with multiple contradictory plot lines.' (From an essay on Bartoli by Hilmar Schmundt.)

14. *Novio* is the Spanish word for boyfriend but given that the sound of the 'v' in Spanish is more like an english 'b' it sounded like *knobio to* me. *Knob* for short. That was back in the seventies. Punk hearing.

14. This is Gaby Salter. Not just a pretty face, her beauty goes deep and her shamanic powers move even the most sceptical. Once, while she was giving me a healing, I heard uncanny depths of voice and such powerful exhalations that I thought an old man was sitting behind me. I came through the experience feeling that unknown quantities of ancient miasmic goo had been syphoned off by an angelic heavy-breather. I looked round to check she was still there. She was. She gave me a photograph of a beautiful Indian mystic who had come to help. Gaby has also been bringing up the past lately. She said: 'we all had such a lovely time,' when recently she saw a photograph from the eighties of all the children, and started to cry. I said: 'No we didn't,' and started to laugh. We did and we didn't. And now we are grannies we do and we don't, but I always love my beautiful friend.

15. Paul Scully was a sound man I knew on the road between 1987 and 2013. A brilliant sound engineer of course, and cause of much joy.

17. Joe. AB identified three Joes in *Pushing 60* and suggested it might be good to identify them to avoid confusion. This, the first one who gets a mention, is Joe Strummer (born Mellor), a particularly good friend as the other half of Gaby, and father of Jazz and Lola. He once told me he was Joe short for Joseph, but he was really John. Then there is Jo (without an 'e') Finer, Jem's uncle, who died aged 95 in 2002, the same year as Joe above. Jo Finer's legendary storytelling even gets a mention in the *British Medical Journal*: 'He had a phenomenal memory and could relate innumerable fascinating tales of what are now

episodes of medical history.' Jo Finer told us that he and his mother thought he might fit in better if he had a more British name. He said he considered the name Jarvis. The third Joe is Joe Hales, who is the father of Max and Sammy, my grandsons. Incidentally, Max was the name of Jo Finer's father and Sammy the name of his brother, Jem's father. Joe Hales is a brilliant designer who gets a mention in passing but should get much more. He is a much loved member of the family, the outlaw, Joe C Hales. Also originally a Joseph. Two Josephs and a John.

25. Ambivalent as ever. AB checked I understood the meaning of ambivalence. I replied that I understood the meaning only too well, and told him that the line was meant to be funny.

34. Imre Goth was a close friend of my father's, and my mother. He and my father had flying and inventing in common. We used to visit him in Talgarth Road most Saturday nights. I listened to the pilots endlessly into the small hours, while my mother slept on a bed behind the screen in Imre's studio. As a child I wondered why there was a bed there. My mother was one of the few women Imre painted who did not succumb to his charms. Maybe this was why he was endlessly enthralled by her and hung their portraits facing each other in a corner of his studio. One of his more amorous self-portraits appeared to eye my mother, a beautiful young girl of 19, from the day it was painted in 1946 to his death almost forty years later. All but the pre-war mistresses were irritated by the *virgin widow*, as my mother called herself. The elderly German beauties who I met in the sixties loved my mother, and I loved them. Imre became a father figure on the death of my biological one. Aspects of Imre's story come in to several of my works, most notably one in which I took his self-portrait to the monkey house in Berlin, which was immortalised in a film by Uriel Orlow, *The Transgenerational Memory of Monkeys* (2007).

36. Brown's, a hotel in Mayfair that was popular with the likes of Agatha Christie, the Emperor Haile Salassie, and George II of Greece but not with my father.

37. Darryl Hunt can be looked up online for anyone who needs more biographical detail. He is a singer/songwriter and bass player. Also plays the Moog. He was in a band called Plummet Airlines that was formed to be in a student film made to support the miners' strike. The band subsequently went on the first Stiff tour. I like that sort of information.

40. Sophie Richmond has never looked herself up on Google. I just did and it says she's an actress. She's actually a poet. I gave her the anonymity of initials, SR like the toothpaste, SR for sodium ricinoleate, but she said she didn't mind what I called her. I checked if it would be ok to put something subversive she had said into print and she was fine with it. I have long admired her nonchalance.

41. I only recently found out the original name of this most original man, not just a drummer but also a wit and a wonderful raconteur, matched only by his lifelong companion and inspiration, the artist Esperanza Romero.

43. Now most well-known for having brought Joseph Beuys and Marina Abramovic to attention, and for first presenting the great Paul Neagu and Tadeusz Kantor. Ricky Demarco can arouse enthusiasm like nobody else. One soggy Venetian night in 2013 he lectured a little group of us in a boatyard near his Italo-Scottish pavilion. He spoke passionately on the genius of Gadda and berated anyone who was not familiar with the greatest of literary innovators. 'Call yourself a modernist' he barked at me. I was a teenage modernist, I thought but couldn't even find voice to say I had once tried *That Awful Mess on Via Merulana*. Then we all went to the jolliest dinner and bonded over our ignorance of Carlo Emilio Gadda and all agreed how lucky we were not to be at the British Pavilion party. Some of us had even been invited.

43. *Vox Box* is the name I have given to the seventies jukebox I am filling with recollections of art as political action in the seventies, the spoken word memories of friends, family, colleagues and teachers. There is more about it later on in chapter 19, *Here's a long and a late one.*

44. Éamon de Valera can easily be googled to check out his details as a real man, leader of Fianna Fáil from 1926-1959, Taoiseach in the thirties and again in the fifties, and president of Ireland till 1973. As for as his appearance in *Pushing 60,* he is a ghost. He comes proposing marriage. My mother did meet him when he was in London in the late fifties and was delighted to have made him laugh. She always thought him very handsome. A photograph of de Valera from the years of her childhood shows a dark-haired young man, studious face with bird-like features adorned by a pair of those once ubiquitous round spectacles associated with James Joyce. Pensive and pedantic.

46. To be specific my mother's friend resembled the great Bert Lahr as he appeared in the *Wizard of Oz*, playing the cowardly lion.

49. EST is the acronym for Erhard Seminar Training, the transformational boot camp that flourished between 1971 and 1984 and was the brainchild of Werner Erhard. When I looked him up just now, I saw he was the man who had told me to wake up.

49. Alan, who paid for me to be transformed, was the pianist at the top of the house. Alan Rowlands was a professor at the Royal College of Music and one of my greatest friends as a child and adult. He was in the house in Oakley Street the night I was born. He has also appeared in my works, most notably in *Flaxman Exchange* (2013), a tour of UCL immortalised by Lucy Newman and Victoria Harwood Kapadia in their film *FLAXMAN* (2018).

51. Jem is Jem Finer, my husband. He can be googled, although much of the information on Wikipedia is wrong and quite a big part of it missing. Me, for example.

51. Kathy B is the actor, writer and director Kathy Burke. I'm not sure how useful it is to know I am with her in my dreams. She and Jem, see previous note, once appeared in a movie scene together in which she played the murderous granddaughter to his vile old man. She coaxed him to drink medicine then hit him over the head with a Mayan art treasure. He toppled off a balcony like Buster Keaton in the best scene of a bad film. I am not sure what they are doing in my dream other than being companionable.

51. The funniest on-stage presence I have ever known, and good off it too. Looking up Kevin McAleer to check the spelling of his name I got sucked into clips and roared out laughing. Jem called upstairs to check if I was alright. Warning, for those who have never seen Kevin McAleer *live*, the flickering clips are but a ghost of his genius. He once turned the camera on us, himself and myself, and asked me questions in his deadpan way. I think he thought my excitability and his stony delivery might make a dynamic discrepancy of sorts. But I turned dark and droll and so, perversely, proved no foil and no fun.

53. Yoko's film of 365 bottoms, also known as *Film no. 4*, was shown in the Albert Hall in 2017, fifty years after it had been banned at that bastion of patriotism and propriety.

According to an *Evening Standard* article of 1967, Miss Herod, the voice of Land of Hope and Glory, and the venue's secretary, objected to 'disrupting behaviour from way-out elements', and Yoko Ono's then-husband Tony Cox announced 'we are so depressed we can't function right'.

53. St Stephen's hospital is now the Chelsea and Westminster. The new hospital which opened in the nineties has big colourful art and a cheerful abundance of light. It's the glassy and classy type, and appeared as a New York hospital in Kubrick's *Eyes Wide Shut*. The old St Stephen's was scuzzy, its A&E a Saturday-night, dimly-lit regular gathering of all sorts. I went a few times, twice on the back of Jem's motorbike. Once for kicking through a glass door — the metal tip on my stiletto shattered the pane and my dancing foot followed. Another time, the lid of a can of tuna severed a space between my fingers and I still have the scars. There were other times escorting friends and trying not to catch people's eyes. This note has got me remembering so many times. Once, my mother and I were there as companions to a casualty when I spotted a friendly old deviant of her acquaintance and exclaimed out loud, 'look there's your friend xyz from Tite Street'. My mother silenced me with a ferocious look, adding 'I'm sure dear xyz would rather not be greeted just now.' He was clearly the bloody victim of a drunken encounter, and could hardly stand. My brother was a porter at St Stephens after his ECT and that's where he met, as a fellow porter, the ex-monk who had been one of Yoko Ono's 365 bottoms.

58. AB commented on *Endgame* being wrong. And he was right. *Endgame* wasn't performed in the seventies at all. But I remember looking into the blind eyes of Hamm and feeling close. I know it was before... before Jem and all that happened to me.

I have just discovered it was on at the Riverside Studios in 1980, so just before Jem, but way after I was working at the chemist... I could have sworn I looked at Nagg and Nell in their bins at the Royal Court. I could have sworn.

In 1973 *Not I* was at the Royal Court, and of course *Krapp's Last Tape*...

I was so taken with Billie Whitelaw that I couldn't live in her house when offered an attic flat in Camden in 1977 in exchange for some babysitting. I was thrilled with the offer till I asked the name of the actress, and when I heard it was her I declared that I couldn't possibly, on account of being a devoted admirer. The girl who wanted to swap with my room in Soho said: 'You'd be perfect, she'd absolutely love you and your adoration. She was really disappointed I hadn't heard of her'

And then there was *Footfalls*, lines of which I have been muttering ever since, now that *was* at the Royal Court, but it hadn't even been written in 1973. I saw it in 1976, I have just found out via Google. I think of ancient mothers and their elderly children and the questions about time, and of course May Beckett remarking that my mother had a sad look for a child. 'I can feel the rings', as they say in *Come and Go*, written in English by Beckett in 1965. I never saw *Come and Go* but performed in it, directed by Jeremy Treglown in 1977. JT gets an unnamed mention as the encouraging tutor who understood why I favoured Beckett over Brecht.

61. MH is the artist Mark Harris whom my mother met in the early eighties and who immediately impressed her. She was taken by his classic good looks and manner. The way he said: 'What a perfect ear' about the baby sleeping on its side delighted her. 'What a perfect ear' my mother would often repeat, lowering her voice in imitation of Mark's. Maybe I should have given him an alias such as Basso Profondo, for obvious reasons, or Winco, on account of him looking like a flying ace. He brought a very fine wine on the occasion of his visit to the sleeping infant in 1983, and my mother said: 'This is a very good wine' as she stirred in a spoonful of sugar. I think they were always rather taken with each other. His sister Annabel was one of the best friends ever to my mother, but reported feeling somewhat eclipsed by brother Mark and his boxes of candy.

61. Paul Jones was a so-called mixer dance, the dancers formed two circles, boys on the outside and girls on the inside. Both the outer and inner circles would dance around till the music stopped. When the music stopped the dancers did too, and would take as a partner whoever was standing in front of them.

63. Debsey Wykes has the most beautiful voice and laugh. We meet regularly to this day and still find amusement in the tiniest things like a nipple appearing through the hole in a leather string vest. Whenever she isn't around I can listen to one of my favourite albums ever: *Some Dusty*, by Birdy.

63. AB put a question mark by 'the bicameral way'. The book by Julian Jaynes which I read in the seventies, *The Origin of Consciousness in the Breakdown of the Bicameral Mind*, relieved a lot of my panic about choosing the either/or of the rational/irrational and also gave me another way of understanding schizophrenia. I have just read that Bicameralism, the

condition of being divided into two chambers, is a controversial hypotheses in psychology and neuroscience, and that Jaynes' use of governmental bicameralism as a metaphor is a spurious notion. All I can say is that it is over forty years since I read the book that gave me a way to understand living with the dead and auditory hallucinations.

64. Silke Thoss. When Silke realised her surname sounded rude in English, she accentuated the crudity and called herself *Silky* Thoss (silent h) and wrote some irreverent country songs to go with her new name and a squeezebox. She was my friend at the Slade in the early nineties. I was, and am, indebted to the Germans for not being so impressed. After a talk by a revered artist, Silke said: 'Everyone boils with water,' another way of saying *the secret is there is no secret*, or thereabouts. Her work is all over my house. I love it, and her. Both she and Mark, the *other* German, have given me the best times, inviting me to be part of their lives and art.

64. TEFL is teaching English as a foreign language, and was once a common enough acronym. It sounds a bit like Teflon, the non-stick polymer. My mother once announced proudly I was doing a Teflon course. I was there to correct the easy mistake.

67. Again there is so much about Mick on the internet, The Clash, Big Audio Dynamite and his extraordinary library/archive, so what can I add? I passed a self-storage depot on the outskirts of London only last week and laughed out loud remembering his comment about *stuff*. He suggested that people visit their stuff in these faraway facilities at the week-end in a way they might once have visited elderly relatives. One of the warmest and most humorous of characters, and so say all of us, including my friend the artist and taxi driver, Hugo Danino. Hugo assesses his passengers astutely. He and I have compared notes on many personages and we both agree Mick Jones comes out with flying colours.

68. Gustav Metzger is another who needs no introduction or note. This is in large part thanks to those who protected and championed him so that he finally received long due recognition. The artist Jo Joelson was one of Gustav's main friends and probably why he was friendly to me; certainly why he gave me an interview for Vox Box. I never thought he was over the moon to see me, though. When I visited him once in hospital on Jo's suggestion — 'Gustav would love to see you' she had said — he told me rather sternly to stay when I said I was leaving, although he had not looked the slightest bit relieved by my company.

Once, in the nineties, he caught me putting an ordinary muesli in my trolley, in Sainsburys Tottenham Court Road, and cautioned me against the inferior brand. He took a deluxe museli out of his own basket and lectured me on the difference. I swapped at once, and not long after that encounter I stood on top of a car that Jem was stripping of its paint and read from the *Auto-destructive Art Manifesto* in impossibly high heels, brandishing the recommended deluxe muesli. The manifesto came from a book whose note on Gustav Metzger included the elusive phrase 'whereabouts unknown'. It was wonderful his life and art ended on a high note. I still have two little grey cakes on a shelf, the icing letters are fallen but you can still read 'Gustav' on one and '90' on the other.

69. Gorka de Duo was a photographer and beauty who accompanied Andy Warhol in Madrid in 1983. In rereading *Pushing 60* I wondered why I had asked Carlos if Gorka was in the club that night with Warhol, then remembered an earlier mention of the eventful evening. On the occasion of his visit in 1984, when he brought his girlfriend in the leather string vest, Carlos told me all about hanging out with 'Andy' and his attempts to introduce him to unenthusiastic boys. He never mentioned the biro drawings then. Looking up Gorka de Duo, memorable star of the movida madrileña, I found that he was/is now living in Berlin and is into pataphysics. Small spiralling world.

75. Kitty Finer is my younger daughter with Jem. A star turn, a painter, dancer, singer, songwriter, bar-maker and great friend who might wish to remain anonymous. She disapproves of writers using their children as subject matter. We both seem to agree that *mothers are fair game*.

77. Ella Finer is Jem and my older daughter, the first-born light of my life who once said she didn't need children, she had me. A voice of reason and clarity. I revere her intellectual and intuitive brilliance. She also protects her privacy and doesn't have any social media accounts, not even instagram, so I'll say no more.

79. I have known Katy English, brilliant sculptor, painter, storyteller and friend, since I was five, so we remember many real and unreal times alongside each other. She feels bad for appearing as an inattentive and occasional listener to the original broadcasts of *Pushing 60*. She has promised to buy a copy of the book when it comes out to make amends. She also gets a mention for escorting my mother to an evening by the river to see a paper boat float

on the Thames. Katy could be heard talking about her great uncle Jack White, co-founder of the Irish Citizen Army and free love advocate, in a work I made to haunt Byron's bedroom in Newstead Abbey. She also played a lodger in the live soap opera *The Londoners* (2005). Katy's memories of performing in my production of *The Emperor's New Clothes,* down to pants and a chill-proof vest, in 1967, are still quite unpleasant, but she has contributed very generously to my works ever since.

82. 1946-1971: this could confuse readers. AB thought my brother might have died for real in 1971 but he, my brother, was making a point that the ECT killed him in 1971. He remains alive to this day.

83. Sybil Thorndike. You can see her defending Marilyn Monroe on an ancient black and white interview on YouTube. I love that the great old actress suggested that anyone who had difficulties with 'the darling girl' (Monroe) might have difficulties themselves. I remember her crying out theatrically to my mother across the aisle at the funeral of Katy's grandfather. I found it most embarrassing. 'Darling, darling girl', she bellowed portentously. 'Ignore her,' I hissed at my mother, who was already blowing a silent kiss back at her illustrious admirer.

86. Melissa Scott Miller was recently concerned her paintings were too pretty. I assured her that the ones I have are sublime. I love the lonely night with gasometers that I see every day, an eerie scene, and another, a small oil of Kings Cross at night in which the bright lights warm forlornly. And of course it is Melissa who painted the trees at Childwickbury Manor. Those dense intense trees are not just pretty.

88. Bonzo is the dog we all adore. I waited till I was nearly 60 to have a dog and it, or he, is the dream come true.

90. Richard Goolden is another actor and character, as can be deduced even from the mention of him. He too can be looked up on Google. I read in his Wikipedia entry that he had indeed played Nagg and been a friend of Samuel Beckett as I had thought, and that he died in St Stephen's after being visited by my mother. It doesn't actually mention that my mother was his last visitor. I just thought I would add something you could not read anywhere else.

91. Cecil Brock, for some reason I inherited an unwanted plastic bag full of his headshots, beautiful shiny glossies. One of them rests against my record player. I took this photograph with me when I performed a one-off show *A Tale about a Tale about a Tail* (2007)*,* a paean to sad, bad and mad ageing beauties. I took my record player, a red EP of Vivien Leigh reading *Squirrel Nutkin*, and some drawings Imre had done of her. Imre had called her Lillian Vee and was not as taken with her beauty as I was. It still upsets me that I 'lost' Imre's drawings that night. It also upsets me that I can't find any of Cecil's essays on the stars. My mother always said Cecil did well with Gillette. I can't find him among all the blades, all the long gone shavers immortalised in advertisements for another age. One curious shaving ad has a baby holding a razor to its foam beard, but there isn't one of our dear friend. I look him up and under his name it says 'Irish actress'.

91. O'Hara or O'Sullivan. I only remember it was the one who got the part of Esmeralda in *The Hunchback of Notre Dame* and not the one who played Jane in *Tarzan*. O'Sullivan is the more famous of the Irish American Maureens, but AB hadn't heard of either. O'Hara was/is the one who got on the tram.

95. *The Londoners* was a live soap opera performed over six nights at Toynbee Hall. The history of a boarding house in London was based on the true-life psychodramas of my family before and after my birth. It was distilled by Tom Chick into his wonderful 2018 film. Kitty was so amusing and convincing in 2005 as an acerbic old person that an elderly member of the audience was disappointed to find she was in fact a young one.

100. Arding and Hobbs department store in Battersea was where I first saw Father Christmas and sat on his knee. And where my father took a loaf of sliced bread and tried out every single toaster, much to the manager's irritation. Many burnt the toast, some shot slices out across the shop floor, and in one case a toaster burst into flames. Only one worked as intended.

102. Lots about the Profumo affair all over the internet. I heard the name Profumo as Perfumo, like perfume with an O on the end, and found it rather exotic. My friend Claire asked her mother if she could be taken to the fair that everyone was talking about. Discussion about it was everywhere. It seems to have continued to be a riveting subject.

105. The friend here mentioned is Suzanne Moore. We go back a long time, before all the things happened that are now used to describe people. She is well known as a writer but long before she was a household name she invited me to go to a writing class with her. I've always loved her for that and plenty more.

113. Maria Donska was a virtuoso concert pianist and extraordinary woman, a bit terrifying to me as a child. Sculpted by Jacob Epstein and loved by Mark Gertler, she lived for fifty years with Leonora 'Baba' Speyer, the love of her life. Maria was heroic. I loved her impatience and irritation with my grandmother and her distaste for Rachmaninov, whose music she detested. Baba, on the other, hand was enchanting, as if her life growing up to the sound of music in a home visited by Debussy and Grieg, had given her endless ease and charm. Maria's escape from Poland and the fate of her beloved family caused her genius to burn fiercely. I was moved by the marriage of two extraordinary women. Maria's favourite soap, so I learned on Alan's last evening alive, was 'Blenheim Bouquet'.

114. Rupert Sheldrake, now possibly better known as the father of Merlin-Entangled-Life-Sheldrake, is a hero of mine on account of morphic resonance. I just wrote a fact-checking text to my brother in Canada, and this is what he replied:

Yes Rupert was there… the sage was Bede Griffith, an English Benedictine monk, more of a saint than a guru… he gave me a beautiful blessing and granted me a hermitage out of the ashram in a eucalyptus grove. The place was called Shantivanam and I loved that Rupert had written his first thesis on morphogenetic fields there…

I then sent my brother a recording of a discussion about angels between Bede Griffiths and Rupert Sheldrake, and he answered:

Funny to hear the posh voices of Bede and Rupert and what are they saying? Honestly it's all getting to be blah blah to me… don't mean to be rude but fuck it, enough's enough. And that does exclude you… nothing wrong in being frankly partial: your rather marvellously self-destructive honesty is right on… this whole shit-heap of thought-form association is due to blow soon anyway… here's to it! And to you.

This communication thrilled me, so much so that I read it out loud to my revered old teacher Stuart Brisley, and was so pleased that he received it well with laughter. My brother's psychedelic wisdom is coming in haikus from the end of the world just in time to make no sense in a most helpful way.

124. Laozi or Lao Tzu, or Tze, even. AB suggested I might change to the better known Taoism or Daoism but I like the name Laozi and besides a *laozi life* sounds a bit like a *lousy life*. It is also significant and pleasing to me that he might not have been real at all. Ever. His dates are vague; 6th to 4th century BC, and his rumoured birth at the age of 62 and life span of 999 years are in the realm of divine absurdity. I also like what I know of the teachings which were revered by those on the libertarian left, and of course anarchists like the superbly named Rudolf Rocker. I am struck by one proverb, in particular among the many inspirational instructions online, 'to lead people, walk behind them'. This is one of Laozi's sayings that is unfamiliar to me and yet its message is already one of my favourites. It is exactly the same instruction as the one in the old racist joke where the Irish porter says 'follow me, I'll be right behind you'. I always heard the existential wisdom in that so called joke and even see I included it in my musings on Laozi and my father back in 2017. The porter expresses the greatest intention or invitation a leader can offer. A lot of Laozi's sayings have been drained of meaning by being plastered all over tea bags, mugs and fetishised health foods, but they still make sense to those who have issues with authority.

143. Esmonde Robertson. I looked him up and found nothing except for a mention as the younger brother of his more famous sister, Olivia, the high priestess of Isis. He wrote a book on Mussolini, as did Jem's uncle Herman. So many connections in this constellation of great characters I have known and not known.

145. Mark Noll is brilliant in every way, sculpting, cooking and drawing bananas. He lives in Hamburg and Athens and has given me many of my best ideas.

146. Olivia can be found all over the internet. After Mark and I visited, I went back for more. This further encounter of 2007 was captured by Judith Goddard in her film *An Esoteric Afternoon*. Olivia was most enthusiastic about the film and the chapter on it in the book that accompanied the project *12 Shooters*. I suggested to Alex Farquharson, then head of Nottingham Contemporary, that I might invite Olivia when I presented *12 Shooters* there. Alex was enthusiastic, and Olivia even more so. She was straightforward

about her fee, travel expenses and accommodation needs. Nothing airy-fairy about the plans. Alex was keen. I was keen, then suddenly it didn't feel right. It seemed like exploitation. I didn't want to exploit her. Of course she was tough, and a cultivated mischief-maker according to my mother, but she had always praised my aura, and that meant a lot. I cancelled the conversation much to everyone's disappointment and instead gave a talk on the use or abuse of eccentrics. There was a Diane Arbus exhibition on at the time.

148. Judith Goddard is another with a Wikipedia page that gives away nothing of her genius. Olivia called her a goddess and enrolled her at once in the fellowship of Isis. I still have the certificate, as it happens. She is known for video, exquisite juxtapositions of still and moving images, but is also an extraordinary gardener and storyteller.

152. The McEgan always sounded funny, but 'That was his name' said my mother solemnly. 'Did you call him "The"', I asked her but cannot remember the answer, too late now. I looked him up and his name was Darius. AB had not heard of him, but I doubt that many have. The MacEgan does, however, have an online presence. I read in one of the entries that in 1916, around the time of the Easter Rising he adopted the ancient family name 'The MacEgan', unused since the seventeenth century. '

My mother always assured me it was a distinguished name, which made it seem all the more hilarious. There is a self-portrait of him online in a black smock with a big white collar. It looks like he has a good eye for himself, especially his nose. A good eye for a nose, a very big nose indeed. I can see they run in the family (Ha!).

155. Heather Woodbury who I met when she was an underage go-go dancer in New York is a truly great author and performer, a stand-up novelist and extraordinary letter writer. She has brought me back from many a brink via the written word as has the filmmaker Tracy Drew who is a wonderful painter, and writer of images that create indelible visions.

155. Jazz and Lola are the beloved nieces I never had. When they were little, alongside Ella and Kitty, they gave us parents honorary kinship; Jem and Gaby were brother and sister and Joe and I were siblings too.

The girls are still as brilliant as ever, and even more so. One of the perks of getting on is witnessing the once-babies growing into glorious girls and wonderful women. Corny, but true.

158. Uriel Orlow comes to mind in a huge rush of appreciation. A brilliant artist and friend. When we first met I told him about Imre Goth and how he, Imre, had been part of a double agency, how he had painted high-ranking Nazis while being active in a resistance group that helped endangered citizens out of pre-war Berlin and into Switzerland. Uriel told me that his great grandparents were on the receiving end. So it was no surprise that we ended up revisiting an old performance of mine that drew on Imre's life story and escape from Germany. When I found it emotionally overwhelming to go back to Imre's studio for the sake of the film, Uriel reminded me that it was important to do it not *despite*, but especially *because*, it was almost unbearable to do. He put it better than that, but I think of it often, just as I think of elements of the stories from his works. Elegant compassionate work, and person.

168. Jessica, my sister-in-law, is now retired from her tireless work as a primary school teacher. For the last years of her career she was head teacher of a school near where my mother ended up living. My mother said she would sometimes walk round the corner just to see Jessica's name up on the board outside the school. Everyone loves Jess.

182. AB queried this, which was hardly surprising as I had spelt geyser as geezer just to add to the confusion. The second definition for geyser, after the spring that spurts intermittent jets of hot water and steam, is *British: an apparatus for heating water rapidly with a gas flame (as for a bath).*

195. Peggy is one of the most brilliant sculptors and characters I have ever known. When we were colleagues she would drive me to and from work, the happiest journeys, and I only have to hear someone calling another 'babes' and it brings it all back.

202. Philip Carr-Gomm is now listed as the former chief. He handed on the role of Chosen Chief of the Order in 2020. When I look him up I can't help but notice a course being advertised: *The Garden of Flowing in Perpetual Happiness, Coming Home to Ourselves, FREE.*

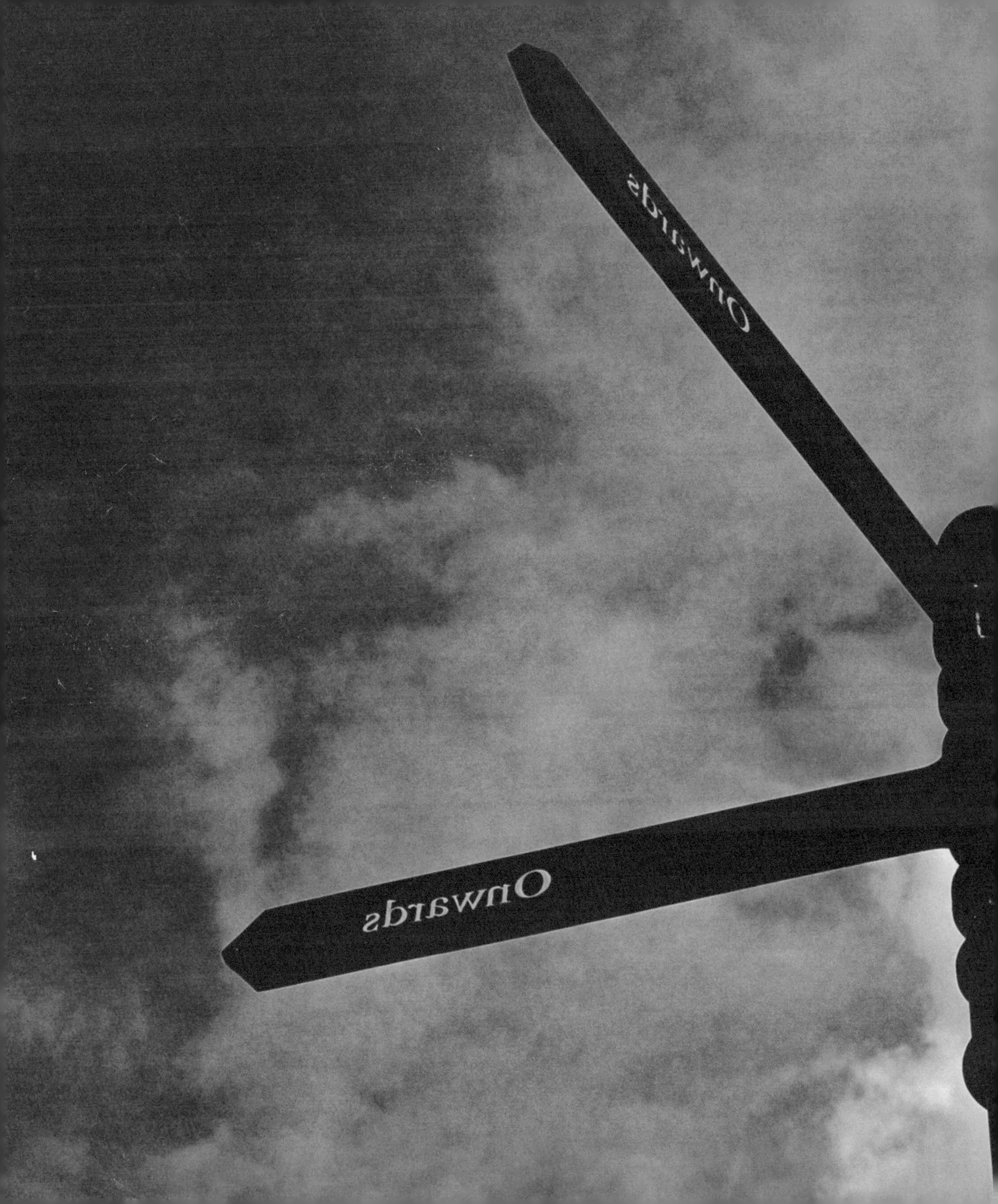
Onwards
Onwards